Gift of Rev. H. Galuszka

MARY WAS HER LIFE

THE STORY OF A NUN

Sister María Teresa Quevedo

1930-1950

by SISTER MARY PIERRE, R.S.M.

Copy 2

BENZIGER BROTHERS, INC.

New York, Boston, Cincinnati, Chicago, San Francisco

NIHIL OBSTAT:

William E. Maguire, S.T.D.
Censor Deputatus

IMPRIMATUR:

✠ George W. Ahr, S.T.D.
Bishop of Trenton
July 24, 1959

MARY WAS HER LIFE: THE STORY OF A NUN: SISTER MARÍA TERESA QUEVEDO.

NO. 2770

LIBRARY OF CONGRESS CATALOG CARD NUMBER: 60-9445

For Our Lady of Lourdes
To Whom I Owe
So Much.

Contents

Preface

TERESITA Quevedo (known in Religion as Sister María Teresa), whose life this book brings to the English speaking world, will captivate many hearts. Readers will be impressed by the story of her spiritual life, which is told in a most gentle, absorbing and delicate style, as well as with a fitting modern touch, by Sister Mary Pierre, whose years spent in Spain revealed to her the richness of the spirituality of Teresita.

The life of Teresita in the world was very brief; at the age of twenty she closed her eyes in death to behold then the loving gaze of her *Madre* (as she was accustomed to call Our Lady) who lived so vividly in her life. In that short span of time Teresita accomplished her mission and left for study a model of holiness which can easily be imitated. Hers was the little way to sanctity, namely, holiness obtained through a rich, vibrant and tender love of Our Lady. From her early years she experienced a special grace which enlightened her mind with a deep knowledge of Mary and inflamed her will with a desire to conform her will with that of her heavenly Mother.

When Teresita in all innocence explained to her spiritual director her life in Mary and asked his permission to consecrate herself to Our Lady according to the teachings of the True Devotion, he remarked: "You have been living your own true devotion to Mary." Upon his advice, therefore, at the youthful age of thirteen, Teresita consecrated herself to Mary according to the formula composed by Saint Louis de Montfort.

In his explanation of the True Devotion, Saint Louis notes that, while many may consecrate themselves to Mary and keep the external observances of the devotion, it often happens that the essence of the consecration, namely, the interior practices of the devotion, are little understood and neglected. Not so with Teresita! Her consecration to Mary was total, interior and exterior. She lived in such awareness and dependence upon Mary that her spiritual father remarked: "Mary was her life." As one reads her biography the soundness of this judgment is verified. Teresita was truly a Marian Soul, a Child of Mary. Her Mary-life is detected throughout the many beautiful excerpts of her spiritual notes; it is evident in the advice she freely, openly and without any fear of human respect, gave to others about love and devotion to Mary; one feels it in her conversation wherein she speaks warmly and lovingly of her *Madre;* it is discerned in the way she lived and suffered, and the manner in which she died. She was a chosen child of a loving Mother who was ever before her and vivified her life.

The knowledge of the life of Teresita comes to the world at a critical time when, to the dismay of right-minded and religious people, holiness, reserve and idealism are cruelly and forcefully being taken away from growing youth, both boys and girls. For them the life of this lovely youthful client of Mary Immaculate can have a special meaning and exercise a magnetic power. Youth is naturally impressionable and revels in ideals and responds to inspirations. Teresita is for them in a most special way; she was all they would want, youthful, charming, gay, attractive, and at the same time a loving child of Mary, one who had asked her *Madre* for the grace that she might never commit a venial sin.

The family life of Teresita is an object lesson for family life today. If our nation is to preserve its strength, its courage, and its purity, together with the priceless gifts of liberty and opportunity for all, the American home must become a nursery of virtue and a school wherein spiritual values are taught by God-fearing parents to their children. Sister Pierre's beautiful account of the family life of Teresita introduces the reader to a true Christian home; from these pages there shines forth the genuine holiness of the parents of Teresita and the bond of charity which existed between herself and her brother and sister. Our Lady was indeed the Mother of the Quevedo home and Jesus was the beloved Father. Many are the lessons which parents can learn from the beautiful spiritual harmony pervading the Quevedo family even though they lived in the turbulent times of the Spanish Civil War.

Most humbly and prayerfully is the blessing of God asked upon this precious book, which presents the refreshing, charming and inspiring picture of a Marian Soul, Teresita Quevedo, Sister María Teresa. May it be read far and wide, by the young and by the old. Its message is the simple message of "to Jesus through Mary." Teresita was a child of Mary, she was totally consecrated to her loving *Madre,* she was ever aware of Mary, she imitated her in her life, and she depended upon her for all things. Our Lady, like a loving Mother, responded and obtained countless graces and blessings for her special child and above all brought her to an intimate and profound love of her divine Son. Mary never seeks herself alone; her gaze is always toward Jesus, and her greatest joy is to bring to Him the souls who have entrusted themselves to her care.

✠ JOHN J. CARBERRY
Bishop of Lafayette in Indiana

September 24, 1959
Feast of Our Lady of Mercy

CHAPTER I

María Teresa Quevedo

WITH the agility of a boy, old Ricardo mounted the circular staircase to the belfry of Saint Francis' Church in Madrid. Strange that his customary limp did not retard him! Had the friars seen him, they would have been amused. Many times, when he had been reprimanded for having rung the Angelus late, he had declared that his stiff right leg always hindered him from taking the stairs quickly. However, such punctuality on April 14, 1930, was understandable; for it was not an ordinary day in the life of the aging sexton. Never—and Ricardo had been at Saint Francis' Church for fifty-nine years—had the birth of a parishioner's child been providentially slated to coincide with the Angelus bell. Padre Fernando had just given him that news.

"Any moment now, perhaps while you are ringing the Angelus, the new Quevedo baby will come to town, Ricardo. I have given the mother my blessing."

Padre Fernando was never wrong, Ricardo mused. And todav was no exception! On the second floor of an unpretentious apartment house, not too far from Saint Francis' Church, the cry of a new-born baby girl blended with the dying sounds of the Angelus.

In the church whose bells had heralded her birth, Father Ignatius Navarro, Chaplain to His Majesty King Alfonso XIII, and an intimate friend of the Quevedo family, christened the little girl María Teresa Josefina Justina. Her names honored Our Lady, the Seraph of Avila, Saint Joseph, and Saint Justina to whom her mother had a strong devotion.

María Teresa's father, Doctor Calixto Quevedo, distinguished in the medical field, owned that seven-story apartment house, No. 7 Plaza de Oriente, which is situated directly across the square from Madrid's Royal Palace. No. 7 is the only city home this generation of Quevedos has known; in fact, the doctor and his wife still occupy the spacious second floor in which María Teresa was born.

The Quevedo apartment house, built around a very large patio, is of modern architecture—sober and practical. On the whole, it is not artistic. The patio, however, has been made charming with orange trees planted in great ceramic tubs, magnolia trees, gardenias, hydrangeas, and the red geranium beds which sketch a lively design in the green clover which carpets it.

Perhaps the most attractive feature of the seven-story house lies in the balconies of the façade which overlook the gardens of the Royal Palace. From the Quevedo balconies can be seen the life-size white marble statues of ancient Spanish kings, which accentuate the verdure of the royal gardens and stand as if in admiration of their floral beauty.

These aspects of nature, which had set the background for María Teresa Quevedo's birth, might well suggest a Spain flowing with milk and honey were we not cognizant of the savage spirit that permeated the country in 1930. The soul of

Castile was terrified because the cold war that Communism was waging on Catholicism had long been undermining the country and had now grown hot enough to explode.

What a pity that a girl born with a natural love for the pageantry of a monarchy should be deprived of elaborate spectacles like those her parents had enjoyed from the balconies of their home. Heaven alone knows whether the Quevedos will ever again watch noble guests alight from American Cadillacs, gather regal robes about them, and ascend the marble staircase to the Palace reception rooms. In 1930 that royal era was on the wane. A year later, on Teresita's—as they had come to call her—first birthday, King Alfonso XIII was forced to abdicate, and the Spanish monarchy went with him.

The baby knew nothing about King Alfonso or the dissolution of the monarchy as she lay crying in her cradle.

"The baby sounds hysterical!" Mrs. Quevedo's voice rose sharply as she hurried to the nursery. The granddaughter of Admiral Luis Cadarso of Spanish-American War fame seldom raised her voice. "Daria, where are you?" she called excitedly to the nursemaid as she picked up the baby, whose unusual hiccoughing had brought her to its crib.

"Put her back in the cradle, Mama. Let me show you how she kicks and laughs when I tickle her." The large brown eyes of four-year-old Luis looked up innocently at his mother.

So that was it! How many times had she told Daria not to allow Luis in the nursery alone? And she herself had warned him not to touch Teresita unless one of the grown-ups was present.

"He must not be scolded," Mrs. Quevedo told herself. "Luis dearly loves his baby sister and I must do nothing that would diminish his affection." Soothing Teresita, she turned to Luis and said: "Son, run along to Carmencita's room and tell Daria that I want to see her. You take care of your little sister until she returns."

An appeal to the protective instinct in Luis brought immediate action. He ran to babysit with sixteen-month-old Carmen.

That little trio made up the family of Don Calixto and Doña María del Carmen Quevedo.

"They are happy, healthy children; we are blessed," Mrs. Quevedo wrote to her sister-in-law in Puerto Rico when Teresita was three years old. "Each one, however, is different. Luis has the manner of an army general. Carmencita is quiet and thoughtful; she will probably enter a cloister. Teresita is a bundle of happiness. Everyone loves her. She is the exact opposite of Carmen in every way, even to her golden hair and blue eyes. Pretty as a picture, but terribly self-willed. Perhaps we have indulged her more than we should because she is the youngest. Whatever the reason, she cannot be crossed. We shall have to do something about it."

It was not long before Mrs. Quevedo found the cure for Teresita's wilfulness. She told Doctor Quevedo about it one evening at dinner. "Teresita was playing in the patio this afternoon with Carmen, Luis and the children from the neighborhood. Suddenly she ran into the house, sobbing aloud. I called to her but she didn't answer, nor did she come to cry in my arms as usual. I decided to follow, for I wondered about her strange behavior. Do you know what that dear child did, Calixto? She went directly to her bedroom, knelt before the statue of Our Lady, and wept."

"I suspect, María del Carmen, that the tears may have relieved a bad temper?" Don Calixto replied quizzically.

"Oh, I am ahead of my story, Calixto. I've left out the most important part! Daria told me that Teresita slapped one of the children because he would not give her his toy. A quarrel followed. To punish Teresita, the nurse ordered her to sit on a bench. Teresita refused. Disconcerted, Daria told her that she was the most disobedient little girl she had ever known. 'What does disobedient mean?' Teresita asked. 'It means that you have hurt Our Blessed Mother,' Daria replied. Then, Daria said, she ran into the house as fast as a frightened rabbit. You know the rest of the story, Calixto. Incidentally, she ate very little dinner tonight. Teresita can't bear the thought of having hurt Our Lady. Isn't she a little young to react like that, Calixto?" Doña Maria asked.

"Yes, she is. However, Daria's ignorance concerns me more than Teresita's pious behavior. Just imagine what my Jesuit brothers would reply to her definition of obedience! I must instruct her not to act as a catechist, but to send the children to you when questions of this nature arise in the future."

Perhaps Daria's ignorance caused Doctor Quevedo a troubled thought; but we wonder if the servant's remark might have fallen like the mustard seed. For after that incident in the patio, little Teresita began to make frequent visits to Our Lady's statue in her bedroom. Apparently she prayed in earnest—as pilgrims pray at a shrine.

During this period of her childhood, it was also common for Teresita to steal into her father's bedroom early in the morning and whisper in his ear: "Papa, may I get in bed with you?"

Don Calixto, reluctant to move but unable to resist, would take her in his arms and teach her to pray: "O sweet Virgin Mary, my Mother, I offer myself today completely to you. I beg you to give my body, eyes, ears and tongue, my heart and soul to Jesus. I am all yours, holy Mother of God. Watch over me! Amen."

Years later, a priest asked Teresita how her devotion to Our Lady began. "I believe Our Lady herself taught me to pray, through Papa," she answered. "From early childhood, when Papa taught me to make the Morning Offering, it was always a prayer of holocaust to Our Lady."

In June of 1934, the Quevedo family was en route to their summer home in Santander. They stopped to buy gasoline in the plaza of a small town in the Province of León, where several barefoot ragamuffins were playing at the fountain. Eager to get a good look at the "elite" of Madrid, the youngsters crowded around the car and pressed their smutty faces against the half-open windows. It was Teresita's first conscious encounter with "dirt," and since she was an extremely fastidious child her reaction was violent. She ordered the children to "get away from here."

Don Calixto observed her behavior and he was annoyed; but he waived his annoyance in favor of the tact he knew the situation called for. As they drove on, he explained to Teresita that those children were poor—"Poorer than the Baby Jesus was in the cave at Bethlehem," he told her. "Their poverty makes God the Father love them very much. It may be that they, too, offer their hearts to Our Lady every morning and that Mary loves and accepts their offering just as she does yours, Princess." For the first time since she had learned to talk, Teresita was speechless! Her silence convinced Don Calixto that he had taught her a lesson.

A similar situation arose on their return to Madrid in September, when a group of rough gypsies tried to make friends with Teresita. "Now," Doctor Quevedo thought, "we shall see what fruit my June lesson bears." Teresita fought her antipathy, but she could not force a whole-hearted response to their friendliness. The expression on her little face betrayed traces of an intolerance that had not been utterly conquered. However, she "uttered" no offense. That was praiseworthy. So her good father decided to ignore her displeased expression and encourage the effort he knew she had made.

"We believe Teresita is trying very hard to convert her horror of 'dirt' into a kind and sympathetic tolerance," Mrs. Quevedo told Sister Carmen, Dr. Quevedo's sister, one day when Teresita was five. "She came in after nursery school yesterday with three urchins she and Daria had met in the plaza. It amused me to see her teach them to wash their hands and face. Afterwards, she invited them to the patio where Daria served them hot chocolate and cookies. Their 'hostess' insisted on napkins. I'm sure they had never seen them before, but they were patient pupils. When the time came for the children to leave, Teresita gave each of them one of her treasured toys. Sometimes I wonder about Teresita, Carmen; she seems unusual for her age. She is different from Luis and your little namesake. But don't misunderstand me, they are precious children, too. It is the unique things that Teresita does that makes her unlike the others."

Carmen Quevedo associates Teresita's early years at the family dinner table with a vehement expression of: *"No me gusta."* (I do not like it.) She was a finicky child, and refused many tasty dishes served in their dining room. Teresita preferred to choose her own diet. Realizing that wilfullness played a far greater role in this than the child's palate, Don Calixto set about to correct the fault. He explained to her that food is one of God's gifts to us—that it helps our soul grow in love of God, just as it gives strength to our body. Unfortunately, he added that we should eat "whatever agrees with us." Teresita absorbed the explanation. The following day at dinner, she declined a serving of soup with an impish smile, saying: "No, thank you, it doesn't agree with me." And a charmingly evoked "It doesn't agree with me" carried her through what might have been many a mealtime struggle with her parents.

When the Quevedo girls went to Our Lady of Mount Carmel Academy, the noonday meal was served to the day students. Carmen feared what she knew would be her sister's fate if she tried her "It doesn't agree with me" on the Sister in charge of the dining room. Apparently there were no "battles," for some months later, Carmen's curiosity having risen to a peak, she asked Teresita how she liked the meals. Her little sister declared triumphantly: "I'm really learning self-control, *Chatina.** I heard Sister Mary Teresa tell the eighth-grade proctor that girls her age ought to be controlled. I decided to get off to a start by eating whatever they serve at meals. I think I'd like 'to be controlled' by the time I reach eighth grade."

Evening Rosary had for generations been a Quevedo family custom. Before the children would retire, Tía Josefina, Mrs. Quevedo's aunt who lived with them, and the Quevedo quintet would gather around a beautiful wood carving modeled after Murillo's Immaculate Conception. It stood on a pedestal in the foyer off the main parlor. Kneeling in the soft light of two blessed candles, the group would follow Don Calixto through the prayers for the decades of the day. Teresita had not missed an evening Rosary since her fifth birthday, but tonight, April 14, 1936, she was putting up a desperate fight against the temptation to skip off to bed unnoticed. The suspense that cloaked her sixth birthday party had fatigued her. Besides, rumors of the war that was devastating their beloved Madrid had excited her. In spite of the somber shadow cast upon normal family living, Don Calixto had in-

* Her pet name for her sister Carmen.

sisted on a quiet party for his youngest child. It was quiet, for merrymaking was neither possible nor desired. That is why Teresita's golden head began to nod after she had consumed the last morsel of her portion of orange chiffon birthday cake.

"I was exhausted," she has said referring to that incident. "I fought hard to overcome sleep until we had said the Rosary. However, only minutes before it was to begin, I gave in to an overpowering temptation. Hoping no one was watching me, I tiptoed to my room. In the twinkle of an eye, I had exchanged my party dress for pajamas. Then I knelt before my statue of Our Lady and whispered, 'I give you my heart and my soul, dearest Mother Mary,' and hopped into bed. As I turned to put out the lamp on the night table, I saw Papa pass the doorway of my room, carrying his Rosary. I felt guilty, so I called: 'Papa, I have not said the Rosary today, but I am terribly sleepy.' He came back to the doorway. '*Bueno,* Princess, say a Hail Mary and go to sleep. I'll offer the Rosary for you,' he said. Dear Papa always knew how to put his princess at ease."

From those early days, the Rosary was Teresita Quevedo's favorite devotion. As she grew up, she taught Daria and the cook to say it. Many of her school friends have told us that they found her fidelity to the daily recitation of the Sorrowful Mysteries, in the presence of the Blessed Sacrament, an inimitable practice.

In January, 1937, the scathing Communist blows against Madrid caused Dr. Quevedo to move his family to the North of Spain. Their summer home on the Cantabrian seacoast would be a much calmer place to live, at least for a while. Mrs. Quevedo did not question her husband's decision and made immediate preparations for their exodus.

Before dawn, the family set out in their blue Buick on a

morning that was exceptionally cold for Madrid. Toward noon, after having stopped several times along the way for hot coffee or chocolate, the imposing site of Santander came into view. On a wide curve in the road, nature presents a thrilling mountain-sea spectacle of unforgettable grandeur. Dr. Quevedo pulled off the highway; he wanted to take in its winter beauty.

"Breathtaking, isn't it?" he remarked. Then he went on as if he were rehearsing lines for a drama. "What a comparison one can make between this majestic mountain beauty, this tumultuous Cantabrian Sea and the placid, blue Mediterranean atmosphere of the Costa Brava. If I had listened to your father, Maria del Carmen, . . ."

"We would have bought a summer home in the Province of Barcelona. Yes, I know the story, Calixto. I've heard it a hundred times."

The children cheered their mother's quick wit and praised their father's good judgment. Meanwhile Don Calixto pulled out on the highway and headed the car for the snow-capped mountain.

The Quevedo home in Santander was situated in the geographical center of the province in a town called Barriopalacios. It is reputed one of the most picturesque spots in all of Spain. As the Buick approached their rambling, greystone mountain house, Don Calixto could see Paco the caretaker reading a thermometer that hung to the left of the front door.

"Terribly cold day, Paco," Dr. Quevedo said to the man, who had rushed from the porch to greet the family.

"Not too cold, Señor, not too cold." Paco had a habit of repeating. "We have been suffering zero weather for two weeks. Today she is only two above zero. Last week she fell below." Paco always used inanimates that were changeable in the feminine gender. "Don't fret, children, don't fret. The sun will appear this afternoon," he prophesied as he began to unload the trunk of the car.

"At two above zero, the sun won't do much warming up, Paco," Luis said.

"Well, maybe not, Señorito, maybe not. She may not satisfy the cold feeling, but, good lady that she is, she will gladden the heart when she smiles down on us." Paco picked up two large suitcases and went into the house whistling Verdi's "Anvil Chorus."

"I have never been here in mid-winter, Calixto." Mrs. Quevedo sounded apprehensive. "You don't think we've made a bad move, do you? The place is terribly barren. What are the children going to do without their usual forms of recreation, with no flower garden, and with nothing but leafless trees in the orchard?"

"I'll tell you what they are going to do, María," Don Calixto answered with a twinkle in his eye. "They are going to get down to business at ten o'clock tomorrow morning. I wrote ahead to Don Fulano at Santander College. One of his tutors will be here every day, starting tomorrow, from ten to two. She will teach Luis and Carmen. As for Teresita, I'll let you know this evening how she is going to occupy her time."

"I should have known, Calixto . . ." Doña Carmen smiled.

After lunch Dr. Quevedo drove off, leaving Mrs. Quevedo and the children behind to unpack and arrange their personal belongings. He returned for the evening meal and announced that he had spent the afternoon with his brother Antonio Quevedo, S.J., who, incidentally, had sent them his love and a blessing.

Turning to Teresita at the dinner table Dr. Quevedo said, "Your uncle has given me charge of instructing you for First

Holy Communion, Princess, because there are no formal classes being held on account of the war. How do you like the idea?"

"Oh, Papa, I love it," Teresita answered, smiling at her father.

Dr. Quevedo also got down to business the following morning. In the catechetical class with Teresita was her first cousin, Oscar Quevedo, one of the seven children left behind when his father, Manuel, died a martyr's death for his Faith. Oscar was a real boy, masculine to his finger tips. Nevertheless, Uncle Calixto brought tears to the young lad's eyes as he effectively explained the meaning of Confession and Holy Communion. Oscar loved those classes. So did Teresita. Both listened with attention rare in children so young.

Perhaps because of the upsetting times, perhaps for some other reason we do not know, Teresita has left us almost no account of what she experienced when she received Our Lord for the first time. We merely know that she and Oscar received their First Holy Communion on the feast of Saint Martha, July 29, 1937. Teresita wore a simple white voile dress and the customary long, white lace veil. Oscar, at her side, was attired in a white linen suit. The families of both children were on hand for the big event, and Father Antonio Quevedo, S.J., gave them their first Communion.

It must have been a day of mixed emotions—happiness and grief. Such an occasion was bound to reopen the not-yet-healed wounds caused by the death of five heroic members of the family. The absence of those dear ones, we know, was mourned by the grown-ups and we see its sad reflection in the face of poor little Oscar. "The photographer could not coax a smile from him as he posed with Teresita after their Communion breakfast," Father Quevedo tells us.

We do not know what passed between Teresita and her

Divine Guest on that July morning, but of one thing we are certain. Teresita Quevedo must have made various promises to Our Lord, for she never missed daily Mass voluntarily from July 29, 1937, on. Often that meant great sacrifice.

We have learned of another promise Teresita made after her first Confession. Here are her own words: "One day when I was six years old, Mama and Papa went to Toledo—I don't remember why—and we were left with Tía Josefina. Late in the morning, Carmen and Luis were playing in the patio, Tía was sewing in her bedroom, so I decided to go to the kitchen to visit Beatrice, the cook. I often did that when Mama went out.

" 'What are we having for dinner, Beatrice?' I asked her.

" 'We will start with bean soup,' she answered.

" 'Ugh!' I shrivelled up my nose. 'I hate it. Just wait, Beatrice, until you hear Tía Josefina at dinner. I don't intend to taste it.'

"Dinner was served. I could hardly wait for Tía to finish grace, so anxious was I to show my nasty colors. We sat down. The others were picking up their soup spoons when I deliberately pushed the soup plate against my glass of water so as to attract Tía's attention. She turned to me and said so sweetly: 'Take your soup, darling; it is delicious.'

" 'No,' I answered boldly.

"Tía was horrified, but she corrected me ever so gently. I don't know what came over me (I hadn't planned this) but I screamed, 'Stop scolding me! I shall tell Mama and Papa on you the minute they come into the house.' Carmen and Luis were as pale as death. I jumped and ran from the table in tears.

"Poor Tía Josefina! I was the only one who ever disobeyed her. I blush for shame now at the way I answered her back.

She was a very holy person and deserved so much more from me than I have ever given her.

"Usually after such disagreeable outbursts—there were a number of them before I received my first Holy Communion—Tía would watch for the first sign of sorrow on my face. (I never apologized, I am ashamed to say.) Then she would ask, 'Would you like me to curl your hair, dear?' What patience and kindness she possessed! Not a word about my bad behavior to me, nor to Mama or Papa. She taught me many lessons in that quiet way—patience and repentance. Without a word, she forced me to grow truly ashamed of myself. I explained this incident of the 'bean soup' to Father when I made my first Confession. I told him it was one example of many such ugly displays. Father asked me to promise Our Lord a sincere respect for my elders, when I received Him into my heart the following morning. I did. And so many times since I have begged dear Tía Josefina's forgiveness."

Dr. Quevedo saw a change in Teresita after she had made her First Holy Communion. In a letter to his Jesuit brother Antonio, he remarks:

Dear Antonio, . . . Since Teresita has received her First Communion, there have been times when I have had to pray for the light to understand her. The following will give you an idea of the change that has come over her in the past few years. I must say that, although it puzzled me at first, it has ultimately inspired me.

Whenever we are dressing to go out, I have noticed that Teresita no longer interrupts her mother a half-dozen times, as she did formerly, in order to have her dress zipped in the back, a ribbon arranged on her hair, or to have María del Carmen attend to whatever Tere might require of her mother. Perhaps you can understand how impressed I have been to see this child wait patiently until her mother is completely dressed, before she asks her to lend a helping hand. One day my curiosity impelled me to ask her why she always waited until last. Her response overwhelmed me, Antonio. "I do not like to bother Mother while she is dressing, Papa, because it would try her patience. I find it very difficult to have mine tried and I am careful not to try the patience of others."

My humble and sincere child could not understand the tears that rushed to my eyes when she told that to me. They were tears that came from the bottom of my heart. The extraordinary power she has acquired over her quick, impulsive nature touched me too deeply, Antonio. I am sure, now, that Teresita submitted herself utterly to the divine influence of Christ when she offered Him her heart on her First Communion Day. . . .

One afternoon Dr. Quevedo was visiting his sister, who was a nun named Sister Teresa, and who was stationed at the Academy where Teresita attended school. Dr. Quevedo related that incident. Sister Teresa showed no surprise because she, too, had a story to tell her brother.

"Last Monday an occasion arose to teach Teresita a lesson which I thought she needed. Her cousin and she were arguing. I asked her to give in to Nines, even though I knew Teresita was right. She also knew she was right, but in obedience to my request she ceded.

" 'I'll give in because you tell me to, Tía, but I'll keep my own opinion about it,' she said. I suppressed a smile and told her that if she should ever become a nun it would cost her heavily to relinquish her opinion.

" 'No, Tía,' she answered, 'if I ever become a nun I will not be self-opinionated. I'll try to be witty and jolly like Madre Anita. I know, Tía, that it is foolish to be stubborn and peevish.'

"What extraordinary thoughts pass through that child's

mind of which we know nothing, Calixto, until some incident like this draws them from her."

Don Calixto's nod expressed the satisfaction of his heart.

In a letter to a friend in America, Sister Teresa recently wrote of a change that she and the Academy Sisters noticed in her niece, from her eighth year on.

... Teresita showed the first sign of sincere humility of heart quite soon after she had received her First Holy Communion. We (the Sisters at the Academy) were truly amazed at the resignation with which she had come to accept everything that entered her young life. Tere never liked to be chastised and had, formerly, excused her misdemeanors with what she called "good reasons." If her reprover did not accept those reasons, she would show her childish displeasure with a very sharp frown and, perhaps, a few unnecessary words. After she had received Our Lord for the first time, however, she used to take a correction as graciously as a compliment. When it was over, Teresita always expressed her gratitude and smiled—regardless of what she may have been suffering interiorly. Not one of us recalls an occasion on which she manifested hurt feelings or offense, after her First Communion day.

I knew that Teresita was an extremely sensitive child. Anyone with such a delicate nature as hers is bound to suffer from rebukes, I used to tell myself. Finally proof of that came my way. One evening, a Sister friend of mine told me that she had just seen Teresita weeping at Our Lady's shrine in the chapel. I knew that only fifteen minutes before, Mother X had severely scolded a group of the girls—Tere was one of them. I was distressed, naturally, but I made no move to bring comfort to her. By that time, I had realized that Teresita shared her little heartaches with no one but the Mother of God.

I firmly believed then—and I still do—that the day on which Teresita made her First Holy Communion, she chose Our Lady as her sole confidante. As I look back, it seems that every breath she took from that time on was for the Blessed Mother. There was nothing she would not do to please her.... Every child has an obsession, and Teresita's was an extraordinary love for the Blessed Mother of God [Sister Teresa concludes].

CHAPTER II

School Days

With the Civil War behind them and their social and professional life reorganized, the Quevedos resumed their normal occupations in Madrid in 1940. Luis was enrolled with the Jesuit Fathers at Saint Ignatius Academy. Carmen and Teresita were day students again at Our Lady of Mount Carmel, located on the plaza of Saint Francis in old Madrid.

Teresita loved the sunny and attractive classrooms of the Academy. She had a true affection for the girls, devotion and respect for the Sisters. But, oh those textbooks!

"What a shame schools have to have texts," she once said to Carmen. And on another occasion, to Luis: "If it were not for books, school would be wonderful." No bookworm here! She did, however, have a keen intellect and a natural ability to learn quickly. Without much study, she always came out high in her subjects.

Teresita, or Tere as her friends called her now, took a genuine interest in her classmates' work. Frequently when classes were over in the afternoon, she could be found in the "home room" seated at her desk. Surrounded by young friends, Tere would help them with the next day's art assignment. She loved art, excelled in it, and would happily assist the girls in their work before touching her own. This showed a desire of serving others that had been outstanding in Teresita since her kindergarten days. It was universally known, evidently, because one of her classmates tells us that: "If anyone needed help, she wouldn't think twice about asking Tere, because she gave it generously to everyone, regardless. . . . The girls throughout the Academy loved her."

"During the study periods Sister Ramona was often a bit put out because Teresita preferred sketching to class preparation," Carmen Quevedo relates. "One afternoon Sister decided to cure our self-willed Teresita. She put an assignment on the blackboard, then faced the class and said: 'Everyone will do this assignment now except María Teresa Quevedo. She may do whatever she wishes.' Tere was humiliated!"

The remorse Teresita felt for that particular fault never left her. Years later, she said to her Aunt, Mother Carmen: "I must expiate in some way, Mother, all the trouble I gave Sister Ramona during those study periods at the Academy."

On the other hand, those misdeeds did not color the teacher's impression of the pupil. Sister Ramona writes in praise of Teresita: "During the years that I had Teresita Quevedo in class, she was enthusiastic about school activities and respectful toward the nuns. During her first few years, she was perhaps a bit self-willed, for she intensely disliked regimentation. I felt it wise to overlook it because she was a good girl, well-mannered and kind to her less-gifted classmates.

"Her work improved as she grew older, and her assignments were always as neat as a pin. The faculty used to say that they reflected her personal appearance because she was a meticulous person. Invariably when the classes voted for the 'best this' and the 'best that,' Teresita Quevedo was elected the 'best dressed.' Aside from her stylish clothes, Teresita was attractive. I often wondered how she could be as humble and simple as she was, for many a girl with her physical grace would have been as proud as a peacock.

"I loved nothing more than to watch Teresita kneel before Our Lady's statue in the students' chapel. She seemed to be united to the Queen of Heaven, heart and soul. She must have been recollected, for one could kneel alongside her and she wouldn't know it. I proved this one day. For ten minutes I knelt beside her while she said the Rosary. Later in the afternoon, Teresita came into the Art room and I asked her: 'Who was the Sister kneeling on the prie-dieu with you after lunch today?' She replied: 'No one knelt on the prie-dieu while I was saying the Rosary, *Hermana.* At least I don't remember anyone.'

"It was not a surprise to me, as it was to other members of the faculty, that Reverend Mother allowed Teresita Quevedo to make the Academy girls' retreat that year—1941. Many complained that she was too young to understand the matter the priest presented in the conferences. Perhaps that is true, but he did impress clearly on her mind the need of making a resolution. In her retreat notes we see, written in large letters, a resolution that became the fulcrum of her brief life: I HAVE DECIDED TO BECOME A SAINT."

At twelve, Teresita was doomed for a fate she dreaded from her first year at the Academy—she was assigned to the home room of her aunt, Sister Teresa. What made matters worse for the fun-loving Tere was her aunt's position on the faculty —she was Prefect of Discipline.

Teresita's fondest memory of those days under the eye of her father's sister tells of the aftermath of a lesson in History. Sister Mary Teresa had clearly sketched the historical position of Charles III . . . his genealogy . . . his temperament . . . his enterprises . . . his heroic deeds . . . his private life and his family. The bell rang for change of classes. Some students left for Art, others remained. Teresita remained. Sister Teresa stepped out into the corridor to supervise the order. "Zing!" A ball flew through space from the extreme right of the classroom. "Zang!" It flew back again, tossed by one of Tere's friends whose eye was not as expert as her hand. The ball struck an electric light bulb just as Sister Teresa re-entered the classroom. The girls could not decide how much Sister had seen as they watched her take a rigid stance, awaiting an explanation. Finally, a student offered: "We have broken a bulb, Sister!" That did not appear to be at all acceptable. Teresita, who had nothing to do with tossing the ball, perhaps because she was Sister Teresa's niece, stood up and said: "Tía, the bulb was twisted and we were trying to straighten it."

"Well," said the amused but stern-faced nun, "in your home, do you usually straighten electric light bulbs by tossing rubber balls at them?"

Teresita, red as a poppy, humiliated by her Aunt's retort, vowed never to try to clear a classmate again by means of a little white lie.

Sister Teresa dearly loved her nieces, but justice forbade favoritism. She treated Carmen and Teresita just as she treated every other student. Perhaps she was a little more strict with them because her fond solicitude longed to make them the very best—the models of good behavior.

After the noonday recreation, the students at Our Lady of Mount Carmel had a period during which they either studied or embroidered. No recreation. No talking. During one of those silent periods when Teresita was thirteen years old, she and her cousin Angelines were chatting away as Tere embroidered on a large tablecloth. As luck would have it, the jingle of rosary beads announced the approach of Sister Maria Carmen, and Angelines had neither books nor embroidery piece.

"What shall I say?" she asked nervously.

"Nothing," whispered Tere. "Get under my tablecloth." And she draped the huge piece of linen over Angelines, producing a very clever camouflage. Sister passed by and nodded religiously to her serious-faced pupil.

"We attributed our good fortune to the topic of conversation that day," Angelines tells us. "Nearly all our private conversations were about the Blessed Virgin or the Sodality. Tere loved the Sodality, but her favorite topic of conversation was that of Our Blessed Lady herself. One day I asked her about her devotion to Christ. She said: 'I love Our Lord with all my heart. But He wants me to love Our Lady in a special way and to go to Him with my hand in Mary's. My affection for her is like that of a tiny child for its mother. You know, Nines, how a baby clings to his mother's skirt when he is learning to walk? Well, that is the way Our Lord wants me to cling to Our Lady's blue mantle.'

"She said that with an expression I can't describe. Whenever Teresita spoke of Christ and the Blessed Virgin she seemed more an angel than a human being. Exclamations such as: 'I love Our Lady!' or 'Mary is so beautiful!' or 'I would die before I would offend my Mother!' were as natural to her as they were to the mystics who love so deeply."

Generous as Teresita was in helping her classmates, she could never find anyone ready to lend a helping hand with the bugbear of her academic life—writing compositions. Even when she would beg Carmen: "Tell me what to write, *Chatina,* I have no idea how to start," she would meet defeat with the reply: "No, Tere, I can't help you. Our styles of writing are different and Tía Teresa would recognize it if I tried to help you."

One spring afternoon in 1944, Sister Mary Teresa had taught her class a lesson on the simple figures of speech, stressing particularly the simile, metaphor and personification. "For tomorrow," Sister concluded, "everyone will write a composition entitled 'An Excursion.' Please try to weave into it as many of these figures of speech as you can, without breaking the unity of your work."

That evening Tere sat at her desk reviewing the excursions she had taken the previous summer. They were enjoyable, of course, but not composition material. She tapped Carmen's vein of inspiration but, as usual, found no flow forthcoming. Her parents were out. Luis wouldn't have an idea in a hundred years. Nothing to do but struggle!

Teresita Quevedo never struggled *alone.* She had a little picture of Our Lady which she used to put on her desk when studies were difficult. Tonight they were about as difficult as they could get, so Teresita set the picture of her Lady atop a pedestal of books.

"For some time she gazed at the picture," Carmen tells us. "Then I heard a '*Sí, Sí, Madre mia.*' She turned to me and said: '*Chatina,* Our Lady's eyes have inspired me; I know what I am going to write about.' I was busy with a Latin translation and told her to write her composition and I would read it when she finished."

An hour later, Teresita handed her composition to Carmen. "Stop now, *Chatina!* You will find this more interesting than Julius Caesar," she chuckled. "Please check the spelling and punctuation."

Carmen read:

On the Way to Mass

I was walking along the Prado Boulevard rather early one morning—on the way to Mass at Saint Jerome's Church—and the lace of my saddle shoe became untied. I stooped to retie it and my eye fell upon a beautiful violet, leaning her head on a pillow of moss that covered the trunk of a cypress tree. As I was admiring its deep purple petals, I heard a faint voice ask: "What are you doing here alone, *niña?*"

I realized, to my utter astonishment, that the violet was speaking to me. "I am not alone," I managed to reply. "I am a Christian and a Christian is never alone."

The violet smiled in agreement and I continued: "What a smart violet you are! I knew you violets were modest but I didn't know you could speak!" I looked inquiringly at the flower but she did not reply. Then I said: "As I look at you nestled against that cypress tree I become aware of my own littleness. How tiny I feel standing here in this vast expanse of air! Papa says that the air is the breath of Christ. When I walk alone early in the morning, I think about those words of Papa. They make me feel as if Christ's breath transports me to Mass."

The violet seemed to nod assent. Then she asked: "Do you know what people call me?"

"I have heard you called many names," I told her, "but the most beautiful is humility."

"Yes, I am the symbol of humility. Some poets have also

dubbed me the color of the Virgin Mother's eyes," she answered proudly.

"Which name do you prefer, violet?" I asked.

"That depends. If I bring glory to God as humility, that is my name. If I praise Him more because I reflect the mirror of His Mother's soul, then I am the color of the Virgin's eyes."

The church bell tolled and I knew I must hurry so as not to be late for Mass.

"Goodbye, violet," I said. "I'll see you tomorrow morning on the way to Mass."

"Don't ask me to help you with a composition again, Tere. You don't need any help—you're lazy. You can do anything you want when you make up your mind. I would love to see Tía Teresa's face when she reads this, even though it may not be her idea of an excursion," Carmen said as she returned the paper to Teresita.

"I think Tía will accept it, *Chatina*. Moreover, I have combined Religion with what she taught us in Composition class today. What does Tía Teresa call that?"

"Correlation," Carmen answered, preoccupied again with her Latin translation.

Our Lady of Mount Carmel Academy is always dynamic with enthusiasm, but it reaches a unique peak every year when the month of May rolls around. In fact, motion begins to accelerate on April thirtieth, when the teachers of the five lower grades pin up their habits and—hammer in hand—climb stepladders, each followed by a tack-bearer who waits in attendance on a lower rung with the aplomb of a Swiss Guard. It is considered an honor to be delegated tack-bearer, for it means that you help Sister convert yards of gossamer into a blue sky with puffy white clouds, producing a May setting for Our Lady's statue.

The background finished, Sister lines up as many paper doves as there are girls in the class. Each dove bears a girl's name and, when it is pinned on the draperies around Our Lady's statue, it becomes the little girl's ambassador to the Queen of Heaven for thirty-one days. The dove's goal is the cloud that surrounds Our Lady's head. The degree of its ascent depends upon the momentum provided by the merits accrued from lessons well known and good behavior.

"Teresita was electrified during the month of May," her sister Carmen relates. "The dove that bore her name scaled the clouds as the month wore on. May was the only month of the year during which she could not be surpassed, not even in class work. Everyone remarked it! She wouldn't open her lips on line, even if Sister happened to be distracted—a moment everyone took advantage of to get in an odd word. Such silence was not Tere's cup of tea. Her supreme mortification, however, took place in the dining room, where she ate with apparent relish what she heartily disliked."

It goes without saying, then, that Teresita Quevedo's dove won the race to Our Lady's heart come May thirty-first.

The devotion to Our Blessed Mother which the Carmelite Sisters of Charity encouraged in their very young charges bore fruit in later years in the life of Teresita Quevedo. When she was twelve years old, she wrote a revealing letter to her sister Carmen, who was recuperating in their summer home in Santander after having suffered a period of serious illness. The letter reads:

Dearest Carmen, I hope you are not disappointed in me. I wanted to write you last week but I have been ill, too—thirteen days in bed. I believe Mama has told you.

Chatina, I miss you very much! Do you at times wonder what is going on at school? Nothing extremely interesting! Sister

Teresa set up the merit posters the first of the month. I don't have to tell you how we feel about them! I didn't do so well last marking period. However, I am going to do better this time—May—for Our Blessed Lady. There are three blocks to star on this year's chart: one for conduct, another for class work and the third for chapel attendance. The stars are pasted in the blocks every Friday as usual. I intend to get three gold stars every week if it kills me. You see, I have figured something out, *Chatina*. There are four weeks in May and if I get three gold stars each week, I can make a "crown of twelve stars" for Our Lady. Do you think she will like that? When I crown her on the thirty-first—in my heart, of course—I will ask her to make my *Chatina* well and to send her home to me soon. I shall also pray for a greater love of Jesus for you and for myself.

I asked Sister Teresa if I could go to chapel fifteen minutes every morning this month before the Mass begins. I had hoped to make that Marian meditation with the High School Sodalists. Sister says I am too young. Instead, she is letting me sit in class next to 'you-know-who' for the month. Tía knows that that girl is unkind to me. I know it won't be easy, for at times she terrifies me. But since it is the month of May I am eager for opportunities to prove my love for Our Lady.

I make a daily visit to Our Lady's shrine for you, *Chatina.* I hope you pray for your little nuisance who loves you very much. Please write me when you feel stronger. I am lost without you!

Too tired to write more. Good night, *Chatina,* and God bless you!

Your affectionate sister,
Tere

The Carmelite Sisters of Charity have the custom in their academies of reading for ten minutes during the noonday meal throughout the month of May. Usually girls have to be drafted into this service, for it is not popular. No one ever heard of a student soliciting the "ordeal" until the May of 1945 . . .

"Good morning, Teresita. What can I do for you today?" It was the Sister in charge of the students' dining room who greeted her.

"Good morning, Sister. I came to see you about the dinner reading on Our Lady during May. Tomorrow is the first."

"Did your aunt send you, Teresita?" Sister was a little puzzled. It couldn't be that Teresita was volunteering to read in the dining room! Everyone knew she dreaded reading aloud for ten seconds. How could she manage ten minutes?

"Tía knows nothing about this, Sister. I have come to volunteer for the first week," she answered meekly. "I want to begin Our Lady's month by expressing my love for her through sacrifice and I can't think of anything that would cost me more at this time. May I read, Sister?"

"Of course, Teresita. Take the book with you now; each day's reading is marked," she said, handing it to Teresita.

"Will wonders never cease?" Sister muttered as Tere hurried off to chapel to prepare for her self-inflicted punishment.

We know that Teresita fulfilled her sacrifice, but she has made no comments on the battle she waged to do so. She seldom remarked her mortifications and self-sacrificing acts, for she was quite uncommunicative about that phase of her life. Knowing this, and with the desire to prove the quality of her obedience, her confessor gave her the unsavory task of disclosing to him the details of her "war over the senses" during the month of May in 1946. Teresita's humility came to the foreground and she wrote Father this letter:

. . . Since you have asked for this report, Padre, I am making it for pure love of Mary. It is in no way meant to be boastful.

The first week of May I managed to overcome myself about eighty-five times, usually through little acts of kindness performed against my natural inclinations. The second week I numbered about the same, perhaps two or three more or less. They were acts of piety, Padre. How many fervent moments I added to my daily prayers! The third week I believe I tipped ninety—mortification was my aim. I denied myself what I like most at meals and ate what I dislike. And there were plenty of opportunities for mortification away from the table! No candy or sweets between meals (so many were offered to me!); no music; and I held my tongue a thousand times when I wanted to say something. I knew that was my best week and I vowed to top it during the last one with acts of Love. Padre, do you know what the most trying penance during the month was? Keeping this "count" for you! I know you will say that it was good discipline. I suppose it was, but I hope you won't ask me to do it again. I prefer to live my life for our dearest Mother Mary without counting the cost.

Another noteworthy incident took place in the May of Teresita's last year at Our Lady of Mount Carmel. On April twenty-ninth, a friend of Mrs. Quevedo paid the family a visit. She brought a bouquet of garden flowers for Doña María del Carmen and a book for the girls.

"I thought this book would interest you and Carmen," she told Teresita. "You are young ladies now and it may have a message for you."

Teresita thanked her graciously. If she had been at all inclined to read that afternoon, the title of their new gift would have discouraged her. *Deciding Factors* awakened no interest in either of the girls.

"Do you think it is a novel, Mama?" Carmen asked, after their guest had left.

"No, dear. It is an educational book, a book on guidance."

That makes it even worse, Teresita thought.

That evening Teresita was quite pensive at dinner. "What is on your mind, dear?" her Mother asked.

"Mama, I have just decided that I can make good use of *Deciding Factors.* I'll read a little of it each day during May. It will be a sacrifice to offer Our Lady. Besides, it will please Mrs. Fulano when she learns I've read it."

I began to read the book [Teresita told her confessor in a letter at the end of May], without any interest whatsoever. Since my will was properly disposed, however, Our Lord gave me the grace to persevere. How good He was, for, there was a "message" in it as Mrs. Fulano said. Several chapters of the book treat of the various vocations in life. When I read the chapter on Religious Vocations I felt that it was written for me. The last line in the chapter asked: "What would you like to have been in life at the hour of death?" What strange means Our Lord uses to send us His Divine Light, Padre! I believe the book has turned out to be my greatest blessing this month.

The organization of Our Lady of Mount Carmel Academy did not provide a varied program of sports for the girls. Yet their basketball courts were adequate and the spirit of their teams left nothing to be desired. Although intercollegiate sports are not favored by girls' academies in Spain, the rivalry that exists among the girls for the interclass championship is highly enthusiastic—more spirited, perhaps, than anything of its nature in other countries. Each class names its team, supports its players one hundred percent, and vies with the other classes to produce the peppiest cheers and to attract the largest cheering squad from among interested relatives and friends.

Before the practice season opened in the Fall of 1946, the members of Our Lady of Mount Carmel's basketball teams were gathered in a lounge off the gym. Their coach, after greeting them and urging them toward a better-than-ever season, announced the various dates for the election of captains and managers for the 1946-47 season.

Less than a week later, Sister Teresa was passing the lounge and she heard shouting that would lead any dignified prefect of discipline to pursue it to its source. What she saw when she opened the door of the lounge baffled her, for the noise had subsided in a split second and Sister faced a group of silent girls. Her niece was seated at a piano, facing her class. She had a piece of sheet music in her left hand and her right hand was raised as if she were about to strike a chord on the piano. Sister's appearance brought the girls to their feet.

"What was that unladylike shouting I heard as I was passing the lounge a minute ago, girls?" Sister asked them.

The coach, her identity lost in an athletic suit which was the same as those worn by the Academy girls, replied: "Neither the girls nor I were aware that a note of unrefinement had crept into the applause, Sister. Do forgive us! You see, Teresita Quevedo was elected captain of her class team this morning and, according to custom, she had to write a new cheer to add to their repertoire. It was the enthusiasm for the cheer of their new Captain that caused the girls to become boisterous. Wouldn't you like to remain, Sister, and hear the girls sing Tere's song?"

A combination of emotions held Sister Teresa's tongue, but she nodded in acquiescence to the invitation to remain and hear her niece's contribution to the cheering squad of "Mount Carmel," as Tere's team was called. Their chief opponents, and rivals for the school championship of '47, were the Sacred Heart team of the senior class.

Teresita sat at the piano again and played the melody of the Toreador Song from Bizet's "Carmen" several times. As she did, the coach wrote the following words on a portable blackboard:

Mount Carmel team,
March on to victory!
Work might and main
To win this game!
Sacred Heart will fight a battle strong and bold—
The Champion title to hold
But we must play to bring, O loyal team,
The title to M. C.

. . . .

The girls sang it straight from their hearts and, as she listened to them, Sister Teresa felt that she had never heard a rallying song that surpassed that of her niece. Finally, Sister rose, congratulated Teresita, praised the team, thanked the coach and left. I wonder, she thought as she walked along the corridor that led to her office, how Teresita will bring Our Lady into this new phase of her life.

That presented no problem to Teresita, for every act of her life passed through Our Lady's hands to Christ. There were no barriers, no exclusions. Her simple spiritual life was not something reserved for the visits she made to Our Lord in chapel. It was her entire life—the way she lived every minute of every day, everywhere. Therefore, her new basketball duties would not be an exception. And if Sister Teresa was not convinced of that in 1946, she must have been later on, when she read what Teresita jotted inside the cover of the notebook in which she kept her basketball cheers. Here it is:

María! Dearest Mother Mary, today's elections mean that I must grow in virtue. Help me to edify the girls on my team. Teach me how to treat them with patience, charity and justice. Since you guide every move of my life, dearest Lady, show me how to use this honor that has come to me only for the purpose of bringing glory to God. You know, my Mother, that I would rather be on the second team than in the limelight, but since the latter is God's choice, I lovingly accept it.

Practice season was coming to an end when the coach lined up the teams for the opening game of the season. Teresita's team grew excited as the day approached. The day before the game, the coach took Teresita aside after breakfast and said to her: "I have done all I can, Captain Tere. You must take over from here . . ." It was customary for the coach, who trained all of the teams, to step aside in favor of the captain on the eve of a game.

Teresita went from the coach to Our Lady and prayed fervently for light. After dinner she posted a notice that requested her team's presence in the lounge at seven P.M.

"This is something new," the manager remarked as they gathered to meet Tere that evening, "I wonder what she wants!" She looked up and saw Teresita entering the room. The captain faced her team humbly. She was confident that Our Lady would speak through her.

"Girls," she began softly, "I called you here this evening because I have a proposal to make to you. I shall preface it by saying that I know you want to emerge from the basketball season with the championship title. So do I. Of ourselves we cannot win it. But we know that Our Lady can win anything for us from her Son—even this championship. Therefore, I would like to propose that we, as a team, consecrate ourselves to our Blessed Mother this evening and promise her to hear Mass and to say the Rosary every day during the basketball season. . . ."

Cheers of approval and enthusiastic "Bravos" interrupted Teresita's words.

"We shall, of course," Teresita continued when the elation of the girls had died down, "carry on the custom of saying the Memorare immediately before we play a game and of offering Mass and Holy Communion for a victory each day that we play for the championship.

"Father will hear confessions at eight in case any of you would like to go this evening. At eight-thirty, he will meet us in chapel at Our Lady's altar where we will make an act of consecration to the Blessed Virgin. May God bless our team and may His Mother lead us to victory!"

Our Lady did lead them to victory in the last game of the season. The final basket, which broke a tie, was made by Tere's team as their class vehemently sang the last two lines of the captain's cheer: . . . . . .

"But we must play to bring, O loyal team,
That title to M. C."

Of all the sports in which Teresita participated—in or outside of the Academy—she loved tennis most. She worked more assiduously to become a good tennis player than anyone ever knew, her mother excepted. Besides basketball, it was the only sport that claimed Teresita as a tournament participant.

"Too numerous to count," Mrs. Quevedo tells us, "were the matches she played through the years, and it was no secret that her interest was motivated by the hope of becoming a champion. Spring in Madrid, Summer in the mountains, Fall in Madrid again found Teresita on the tennis courts a good part of every fair day. Sometimes I wondered how she could persevere in her efforts to excel, for until she was sixteen years old, she emerged from each succeeding tournament close to—but always a little less than—a champion.

"Finally Teresita developed into a top-notch tennis player. Everyone predicted that she would be the champion in 1946 and I confess that I was swayed by that prediction. When Tere returned home the September evening after that final '46 tournament, I was waiting for her in the patio. Her smile and exceptional good humor buoyed me to the pitch of believing that she had brought home good news. 'Are you going to tell me that we have a champion in the family, Tere?' I imprudently asked her.

"Tears sprang to her eyes but she controlled them admirably. With a fortitude that I shall never forget she replied: 'No, Mama. Not the kind to which you are referring. But if you consider one who has won a spiritual victory a champion, then you have a champion.'

"I walked over and put my arm around her; I felt proud and sad at the same time. Teresita sat beside me and told how she had longed, for the past four years, to become a tennis champion before she graduated from the Academy. She had prayed for it and she had worked hard to attain it. According to public opinion Tere was the girl most likely to win that year. It was true—her game was excellent and she went through to the finals. A few days before the last match was played, she told me, one of her classmates met her at the courts and greeted her with: '*Hola,* Tere. I hear you are slated to win the tennis crown. Better warn them to get a large one; a normal size won't fit your head any more.'

" 'That made me think, Mama,' she said. 'I know Conchita was joking, for she wouldn't hurt a fly. However, I could not get the idea out of my mind that perhaps there was vanity in my desire for the championship. Before returning home that day, I went into church and begged Our Lady to do only what would please Our Lord with regard to the final match. Well, Mama, it pleased Our Lord to have me lose, even though I played hard to win today. This evening I stopped again at Saint Francis' to tell Our Lady that I am happy with her decision. There was an old lady begging at the Church door and I gave her a peseta. Wait, *Niña,* she said as I was about to enter, here is something for you. It was a holy card. I thanked her and carried it to Our Lady's altar without looking at it. I knelt, and the card fell from my hand to the floor. As I bent to pick it up, I noticed that there was no picture on the card but rather an inscription in large blue print. Can you guess what was on the card, Mama?' she asked me.

" 'No, Teresita—you tell me,' I answered.

" 'Love makes all things easy,' she said with the strongest expression of victory that I had ever seen on her face."

CHAPTER III

Vacations at Fuenterrabia

OF THE three Basque provinces in Northern Spain, Guipúzcoa is considered the most scenic; perhaps because its dynamic mountains, which look down over the turbulent Cantabrian Sea, possess a beauty second only to that of the Swiss Alps. They, too, are dotted with country chalets whose landscapes and multi-colored flower beds look more like oil paintings of the great masters than living patches of nature. In 1939, Dr. and Mrs. Quevedo went house hunting in those mountains and found an ideal place in a quaint village called Fuenterrabia, in the heart of the Guipúzcoa province.

Fuenterrabia follows the pattern of many Spanish towns; it is made up of the old and the new. Old Fuenterrabia is a fishing village whose proudest boast is a castle which Charles V built in the sixteenth century. The people are typical fisher-folk: poor, rough, respectful and, most of them, honest. The New Fuenterrabia is the vacationers' paradise. Its enormous white-sand beach, known as the most *elegante* in Spain, attracts thousands of bathers during the swimming season.

Dr. Quevedo purchased a two-story summer home that faced the celebrated castle which Charles V had used as a fortress to defend the town of Fuenterrabia in bygone days. Their new cottage was of stucco, utterly white except for green window boxes of pink and red geraniums. There were balconies to the east and to the west. The former faced the plaza of the town, and the latter a mountainside which harbored a shrine of Our Lady of Guadalupe, patroness of Fuenterrabia.

Summer of 1939 arrived and Paco—still their faithful caretaker—had the new cottage as cozy as a cottage can be as he awaited the arrival of the Quevedo family. The only cloud on Paco's horizon was Luis' decision to spend the summer at a Jesuit camp in Santander.

Following the custom of former summers, Tía Josefina took the girls to their mountain home late in June. Dr. and Mrs. Quevedo would join them on August first and remain for the month. Tía Josefina loved María del Carmen's children, and that brief opportunity to mother them was the highlight of her year. However, the "old order" changed in 1939. There were strange goings-on in the Quevedo cottage in Fuenterrabia. The girls had assumed an air of mystery and independence which put their aunt in a mental whirlwind and which, as time passed, threw her budget alarmingly off balance.

Tía Josefina tells us that: "They, not I, took over at Fuenterrabia. My mother had always told me that I had the sharpest eye of all her children. I am sure she would have been forced to modify her opinion had she been there to see the tricks Teresita and Carmen were playing on me. Their subtle misdemeanors had me on the cook's carpet almost every day. I shall never forget an encounter I had with Pila (that was the cook's name) on July sixteenth, feast of Our Lady of Mount Carmel. It was Carmen's feast day. Pila baked twelve fresh peach tarts, took them from the oven and set them in the pantry to cool. She had no more than turned her back when the number was reduced to six. After she discovered her loss, she charged into the living room, mad as a hornet. Pointing an accusing finger at me, she discharged a barrage of Basque accusations which, thank heavens, I did not fully understand. I pleaded innocent, but she did nothing further to solve the disappearance of the peach tarts.

"Another day she fairly took the hinges from my bedroom door as she barged in to thrust a half-empty bread box under my nose. Four of her six loaves of freshly-baked bread were missing as well as two balls of Edam cheese and a pot of homemade marmalade. Where were they? By this time, she knew as well as I. I never quite understood why Pila upraided me every time she found the larder empty. On one occasion, she carried her capers too far and I asked her if she would like to leave. 'Ay, no, please, Señorita; I would die without those two darlings,' she assured me. In Pila's mind there was only one culprit in the house—Tía Josefina."

What did two little girls do with all that food? Carmen tells us that two were not involved. Only one. One nine-year-old carried it to the slums of town in order to treat the fisher-children. They were humble peasants who, until they met Teresita Quevedo, had never tasted such delicacies. The fare of the fisher-folk consisted of fish, rice, beans and goats' milk. Even black bread was a luxury.

Years later, Carmen wrote the following account of Teresita's charity in Fuenterrabia: "Although Tere knew everyone in the village, she preferred the humble people, and her friends were the children of the fishermen, the vendors, and the peasants in general. I remember the first girl Tere sponsored, so to speak; Frasquita was her name. She gave her one of the prettiest dresses she owned, and the girl captivated our hearts when she wore it, for she had imitated Tere's hair style so perfectly that she closely resembled her donor. That flattery inspired greater sacrifice on Tere's part. She looked over her clothes and found a pair of sandals, a jacket, another dress, a sweater and bits of costume jewelry that she could do without because they would make Frasquita happy. That kind of generosity was bound to cause complications, and Tere soon found herself on a spot. It seemed as if every child in the lower part of town swooped down upon her for handouts. I don't know what she would have done if Mama's friends had not come to her rescue. They gave her clothing, food and other useful items in such quantities that Tere never had to turn away a needy Basque. . . .

"I remember so well what the priest in Fuenterrabia said about Tere when she was at the pinnacle of enthusiasm in her charity among the Basques. 'Teresita,' he said, 'reminds me of the buttercup that lifted its face toward the sky and reflected some of the sun's gold, because she, turned ever heavenward, reflects in her small person some of God's shining charity.'"

The letters which Teresita wrote from her Basque home during the summers spent there were characteristic of any normal young girl. They showed simplicity, vivacity, joy and humor. At times they were inspiring.

This letter was written to her cousin Angelines in August, 1943.

Dearest Nines: A thousand thanks for your letter. You must be having a wonderful time at San Sebastian.

Carmen and I are still crazy about this Basque country. The people are utterly wholesome. Yesterday we went fishing with *"Pedro el Pescador,"* as all the children up here call him. It took a lot of coaxing from Carmen and me to get Papa to give in. He thinks the fishermen are too rough for us. Perhaps some of them are, but Pedro is gentle. He loves Our Lady—his Star of the Sea, as he calls her—because she has guided his boat safely to shore during many stormy seas, when others were lost.

Well, Nines, Pedro cleaned his boat for the occasion and borrowed fishing tackle for us. His wife packed a lunch that tasted very delicious after we had spent several hours on the water. Pedro is very generous but, of course, Papa will reimburse him.

I went to six o'clock Mass because Pedro wanted to get off at seven sharp. The sea was beautiful—blue and calm—as we pulled away from the coast. The cuttlefish, however, are very late sleepers, for at eleven o'clock, when Pedro looked my way for the first time since we set sail, we hadn't had a nibble. I think Pedro was ashamed of his fish! Carmen, by this time, was sound asleep, her line limp as a cravat—as Mama always says. It amused Pedro and he winked at me. Then he began to sing. You'll never guess what happened! I felt a nibble, my line began to jump and before Carmen woke up, I had reeled in a cuttlefish. It was exciting! That is the first and only fish I've ever caught! More fun than catching the fish, however, was Pedro's reaction. Nines, he thinks—because I teasingly told him so—that I believe the cuttlefish bite when they hear him sing.

We've had a lot of swimming this summer, some picnics that were fun, and three excursions. We are having a glorious vacation in Fuenterrabia.

Tell me about your pilgrimage to Covadonga,* when you answer this. I would love to go there to visit Our Lady's shrine. . . .

Love to all at your home from all of us here,

Tere.

* Town in Province of Asturias famed for its miraculous shrine of Our Lady.

In 1944, Teresita wrote to her brother in Barriopalacios:

Dearest Luisito: In spite of the fact that you have behaved very badly toward me by not even letting me know you are alive, —a post card would do it!—I cannot let your feast * pass unnoticed. I am offering a novena of Masses for you. Here's hoping all your wishes will be granted, Luis!

What is new in Barriopalacios? Camp life would not appeal to me, but on the other hand, you would find Fuenterrabia dull because there are so few boys here of your age. Do our relatives from the city get over to see you frequently? Nines wrote about your striking coat of tan, so I presume she has seen you recently.

We've had fairly good bathing this season. However, I shouldn't speak too soon, for the rains are about due and if today's clouds are a prediction, we will not be playing tennis tomorrow. Wouldn't you know—after joining the Club and paying our dues!

Carmen lost sixteen pounds and is delighted with herself. You won't know her when you see her. She is, as always, my precious and almost constant companion. She has gone on every hike the Club scheduled since we've been here. I prefer boating to hiking, so while she walks, I paddle the canoe.

Did you hear that María Rese, the famous artist, has a cottage in Fuenterrabia this year? Those rumors we heard in Madrid about her horrible disposition and temperamental flare-ups aren't true, Luis. She is pleasant and generous, too. Last week Mama invited her to go boating with us and we've never had a jollier time. To show her gratitude to all of us for a pleasurable afternoon, she painted a scene of the Cantabrian in my art album. It is priceless! Next week, Comas' grandfather—he is an artist of renown in these parts—is going to paint a mountain scene in it. What a treasure it will be! Shall I will my album to you when I die, Luis?

We are going to Rosa Moliner's birthday party this evening, so I must close now and get ready. You know how the family

* Latin countries celebrate the feast of one's patron as well as one's birthday.

always accuses me of keeping them waiting. I'm going to surprise them this time!

Happy feast day to you, my darling brother! You know I don't mean what I said about your bad behavior. I love you very, very much.

May Our Lady bring my feast-day wishes to you herself!

Your

Tere.

P.S. As you see, my handwriting has not improved!

A year later, 1945, Teresita wrote a letter to her friend Carmen García which reads:

Dearest Carmen: I don't know what you think of me! It has been so long since I've written you but I am not to blame this time. I've been ill. Will you forgive me for not writing, now that you know the reason?

Saturday was the first day Papa let me go back into the swing of things up here. I'm glad it was Saturday—Our Lady's day—because the Altar Society had a *Rosario de la Aurora*. Mama, Papa, Carmen and I attended. It was my first experience and I was thrilled. Mama says these Basques have very strong faith, and I will add that it was evident during the dawn ceremonies.

The procession left the church at seven o'clock—the float in the lead, as usual. Papa says it was a twelve by six foot float—built along the lines of those used during the Holy Week processions in Seville. In the center of the float, a life-size statue of Our Lady—Murillo's Immaculate Virgin—stood in a bed of pink and white June roses and blue larkspur. I was glad they had given Our Lady a touch of blue! On each of the four corners, gorgeous silver candelabras held tall, lighted candles. Papa whispered to me: "It is so beautiful, Princess, I hope it won't distract us during the Rosary." A good warning! I lowered my eyes as soon as the Padre began the Apostles' Creed and kept my mind on the mysteries as best I could. The procession walked up to the Plaza, circled it, and then back to the church for Mass at eight. Papa and Mama walked behind Carmen and me. We all sat together at Mass. It was a rich experience.

Carmen, you should ask your parents to take you to the *Rosario de la Aurora* at your church on the vigil of Our Lady's Assumption. If you ask the Blessed Mother first, you'll be sure to get there.

At six P.M. there was a Holy Hour which closed with Benediction. Afterwards, we four took a walk along the sea and stopped at "The Red Mill" for supper. The day could not have ended more perfectly, for Papa took us to see "The Song of Bernadette" at the local theater. Don't miss it, Carmen; it is extraordinary.

I am enclosing some snapshots I think you will like. Elsa * is not in any of them because she isn't here this summer. She entered the Little Sisters of the Poor in June. Are you surprised? They say she is very happy.

No more news, Carmen. I'll leave you now because my sister Carmen wants to write a postscript. Write soon.

Love,

Tere.

On the feast of Our Lady's Assumption in 1946, Teresita wrote the following letter to her aunt, Sister Teresa.

Dearest Tía Teresa, may Our Lady bless you! Carmen and I have spent the morning of this glorious feast on the water. We went to early Mass with Papa and Mama and, after a light breakfast, Carmen and I went boating. The haze was still heavy at nine-thirty, and Papa hesitated when Carmen asked permission to carry out our plan. He consented, however, when Mama suggested that we row close to shore and that Paco follow us in his boat.

Tía Josefina would not join us because the weather was not promising. Since it was Our Lady's day, however, we felt that the early morning mist might release a late morning sun and,

* Daughter of friends of the Quevedos.

ultimately, a day praiseworthy of the good God who created it. That is precisely what happened, Tía. We got into the boat about ten o'clock and Carmen took the oars, for it was my turn to give out the decades of the Rosary. You can imagine the joy this privilege gave me on Our Lady's feast! We finished the Joyful Mysteries and afterwards we sang all the Marian hymns we have memorized at the Academy. Then I relieved Carmen at the oars and she relaxed for a few minutes before giving out Our Lady's litany. (We had decided beforehand to make our outing one in praise of Mary, Tía.) The litany was finished and we were singing the 'Salve Regina' when I noticed the sun streaming through the mist. Myriads of tiny pastel lights, each a reflection of its mighty parent, ran noiselessly to the surface of the water and was lost in it. Tía, it made me think, and I must have been unusually quiet because Carmen asked me: "Why so quiet, Tere? Are you sorry we chose the water today?"

"On the contrary," I replied. "I am quiet only because I am admiring a picture of grace as it descends upon the soul, if you don't mind a bit of figurative language, *Chatina*."

"Tere, you say the strangest things at times. Where is this picture . . . in the water?" Carmen asked me, chuckling and leaning slightly over on the side of the boat.

"It ends in the water, *Chatina,* but it begins in the heavens," I told her. "Look to your right and you will see the picture I am referring to."

"I've been watching that, Tere, but all I see is the sun trying to burn out the mist. I can't find a picture in that." She sounded impatient.

"I can, *Chatina,*" I replied. "Perhaps you will tell me that my analogy is poor, but to me the sun represents the Sacred Heart of Christ filled with burning love for souls, from which grace flows to us through the immaculate hands of Mary. The white mist represents Our Lady's clasped hands which are parted by the touch of burning Love, and moved to pour grace upon the world. The water represents those who are ever receptive to God's divine grace. And because they are, Our Lady's shower of grace saturates their souls and unites them to Christ, *Chatina.*" That was the best description I could give her of my picture, Tía.

"No, Tere, I won't criticize your analogy, for every time I look out over the water on a hazy day in the future, I shall recall what you have just said. Tere, will you please write Tía Teresa tonight and give her a detailed account of the 'picture' we have just seen?" Carmen asked me.

And that is how I happen to be writing to you this evening, Tía. There are other items I should include here but since this letter is already too long, I'll let Carmen relate them when she writes you.

Much love from Mama, Papa, Tía and Carmen.

Your loving niece,
Tere.

Carmen, too, did her share of letter writing in Fuenterrabia. On September 8, 1946, she wrote an interesting letter to Luis in which she reveals Teresita's enthusiasm for Spain's national sport. Below are parts of that letter.

Our Lady's Birthday, 1946

Dearest Luis, Mama has been wondering if you made the public novena for Our Lady's birthday....

Luis, if you think you are the most enthusiastic fan of the bullfight in the Quevedo family, you are mistaken. Ever since Papa has taken us to the Plaza in Madrid, Teresita has become an ardent fan of Manolete. She reads every magazine up here that carries his performances. And she tells everyone how fantastic the bullfights are. Are you amazed? You have always said that of all the family Tere is the least interested in shows. Well, I began to think you were mistaken about Tere until Papa told me what one of Tere's interests in going to the Plaza is—aside from the fact that she loves the sport and enjoys Manolete. It is not the pageantry alone of the bullfight that attracts her; it is something even more challenging....

Luis, you would not be able to guess in a lifetime what Tere answered Papa when he asked her why she applauds so vigorously when the bull turns frenetically on the toreador, goring him, or tossing him high into the air. As you know, the applause at such moments is at an absolute minimum, yet Tere always claps like thunder. Thank heavens, no one seems to notice her....

I won't keep you in suspense any longer, Luis. This is how Papa quoted Tere to me: "The poor bull always reminds me of myself, Papa, and the *picadores* (the horsemen who incite the bull with spears) recall the legion of temptations that come my way to incite my soul. Like the toreador, Satan has hope of finding me a blind, raging victim, utterly confused—like the bull—when the *picadores* finish with me. Then he makes his final charge to overthrow my soul. Our Lady, however, helps me to toss him into the air, as the bull sometimes tosses the toreador. ...I love to go to the Plaza with you, Papa, because each time I do, I return with a renewed resolution to fight temptations with the strength of a bull—and the calmness of a saint."

I could see disappointment in Papa's eyes because I laughed when he told me that Tere had referred to Satan as a toreador. However, I saw the light of forgiveness when he noticed the tears that her final impressions drew from me....

Luis, please write to Mama and Papa again before we leave Fuenterrabia.... Much love from all,

Carmen.

Aside from the unusual spiritual benefits that Teresita carried away from the Plaza, she must have had a very natural liking for the sport and we know that she harbored a deep admiration for Manolete. When he was gored by a bull and killed in 1947, Teresita was in Fuenterrabia and she told her family that it was a "blessing" that she "did not happen to be a witness of Manolete's cruel death." Shortly after he died, she wrote a letter to her cousin Angelines in which she remarks:

Aren't you shocked to hear of Manolete's death? I can't tell you how it has grieved me. The poor man! His glory did not last long. Recently I met a niece of his who is vacationing here in Fuenterrabia and I liked her immediately. I suppose my feeling was inspired partly by her own charm but mostly because I knew she was Manolete's niece. Please join me in a prayer for him.

"Teresita Quevedo was extraordinarily fond of our regional and classical dances, which she performed with grace and interpreted with poignant feeling," her dancing teacher in Madrid tells us. This interest in Spanish dancing prevented the rainy spells in Fuenterrabia from casting gloom upon the Quevedos' vacation days. Whenever it rained persistently, Carmen and Teresita would don full peasant skirts and soft dancing slippers, and invite the family to the interior patio of the cottage. Paco would clear the floor and arrange the large potted plants as a background, thus providing the atmosphere of a stage. The girls would dance as a team to the recorded music of Spain's best orchestras and to the click of their own castanets.

"They could swing from a *Paso Doble* into a *Jota* with such ease and rhythm!" Tía Josefina remarks. "I was often carried away with Teresita's grace and I shall always maintain the opinion that some of the professional dancers I have seen do not interpret the Spanish regional dances with deeper feeling than she." To that remark Doctor Quevedo is known to have replied: "With you as a press agent, Josefina, Teresita could undoubtedly win fame and fortune should she choose dancing as a career."

Occasionally Don Calixto would take the family to a concert in the city on a rainy afternoon. Or if there happened to be a good movie at the local cinema, they would go to see it. That is, Dr. and Mrs. Quevedo, Carmen and Tía Josefina would. Teresita was fussy about movies.

"A movie has to be good in the perfect sense of the word," Carmen told Sister Teresa one September afternoon after they had returned from the summer vacation. "Tere is annoyingly careful about those she attends, Tía. Whenever anyone invites her to see a picture, she asks what color it is, figuratively speaking of course. At times she embarrasses me. If it has a tint of harmless blue or green—I won't mention red—Tere will not go to see it. A picture has to be pure white to win her approval..."

"Yes, I know that, Carmen," Sister Teresa interrupted. "Even when it is white she says it falls short of beauty. Teresita is unusual in this respect and you will have to accept that and try to avoid being embarrassed by her exactness. I believe the Holy Spirit is guiding her preferences, Carmen."

"I suppose you are right, Tía. Tere is unusual as you say; but in more respects than that one. I have often been reminded of Teresita in the Church History classes that treat of the lives of the virgins and martyrs. I particularly remember that a passage from the life of Saint Gemma Galgani brought Tere to my thoughts. The incident impressed me so deeply I have not forgotten it."

"What is the passage, Carmen?"

"I can't quote it verbatim, Tía, but it calls Saint Gemma 'Our Lady's little gardener.' The passage infers that she walked through life as through a garden. In that garden she nurtured flowers of virtue: joy, obedience, mortification and charity, which she was to present to God's Mother in a beautiful bouquet as she entered her celestial home. Doesn't that remind you of Teresita, Tía?"

"Indeed it does, Carmen," answered the nun.

CHAPTER IV

Child of Mary

THE girls at Our Lady of Mount Carmel Academy made the annual retreat in November, 1943. Following custom, the priest who gave the retreat chose the sixth commandment as a topic for one of the conferences. He began by describing the ugliness of a soul that is tainted with impurity. "Deliberate acts of impurity leave a soul cowardly, causing one to make bad confessions and to receive Communion sacrilegiously," Father told them. "It blinds the spiritual vision to such a degree that a soul can be eternally condemned because of it. Only a few privileged souls are spared the temptations against purity." He concluded his talk with: "Temptations against purity call for a strong trust in the merciful love of God. Pray to Our Lady for such trust every day of your lives, girls. In moments of temptation say over and over: 'Mother most pure, guard my purity.' "

The last day of the retreat dawned. On awakening, Teresita recalled that she must prepare her retreat Confession.

Between the morning conferences she examined her conscience but she could not settle a doubt that disturbed her. Finally she tapped on Sister Teresa's office door. "Tía," she asked, "how does one know if she has had temptations against purity? Father said that those who are spared are few. I am very wilful; surely, Tía, it is impossible for me to be one of the privileged souls that Father mentioned. I am preparing my retreat Confession and I want to make a good one. Will you help me, Tía?"

Blessed be such innocence! her aunt thought. Seated opposite her niece, Sister explained how one knows if she has been tempted against purity.

That evening Sister Teresa wrote a letter to Mother Anita, her sister in Puerto Rico. She related the Confession incident. "I can best describe our niece, Anita, by saying that she is 'like a lily among thorns,' " she wrote.

Perhaps the retreat master had spoken a little over Teresita's thirteen-year-old head when he talked on sin. Not so when he spoke about Our Lady! She completely absorbed every word of his Marian talks. Father told the girls, that for the past five years he had been deeply interested in the "True Devotion to the Blessed Mother" of Saint Louis de Montfort. He practiced the devotion himself and recommended it to others. In fact, he discussed "True Devotion" at the 4 P.M. conference on each of three days. After the first, Father gave each girl a pamphlet that explained de Montfort's doctrine and a few mimeographed articles he himself had written on it. Teresita read all of them.

Immediately after supper, the evening before the retreat ended, Teresita had made a long visit at Our Lady's altar. As she was about to leave the chapel, she saw the tail of Father's cassock swing into the confessional. What could be more perfect! Only five minutes before, she had hoped for an opportunity to talk with him. Again she looked toward Our Lady's altar. "Thank you, dearest Mother," she whispered and went into the confessional.

After explaining that she had gone to Confession that afternoon, Teresita said to Father: "I would like to make Saint Louis de Montfort's Consecration to Our Lady. Could you tell me how to go about it, Father?"

Who could tell her better! However, there were several things of which he had to be convinced before encouraging her to make the Act of Consecration. Father began with: "Do you understand what 'True Devotion' to Our Lady is?" Teresita answered that and each succeeding question clearly and concisely. Amazing, he thought, but I shall make it more difficult. He did, and her response was perfect. Father's admiration for this young girl mounted. When he could think of nothing further to pursue on "True Devotion," he asked Teresita how old she was.

"Thirteen last April fourteenth, Padre," she replied.

"Tell me something about your love for Our Lady. How long have you had a special devotion to her?"

Teresita told Father of her childhood love for the Mother of God. She explained how she had placed her hand in the hand of Our Lady as she rose to go to the altar rail on her First Communion day. And she added that Our Lady still held it.

"The only reply I can make is this: you have been living your own True Devotion to Our Lady. Nevertheless, it will please her if you make Saint Louis de Montfort's Act of Consecration at Holy Mass tomorrow morning."

Teresita knelt in the chapel among two hundred retreatants on November 14, 1943. No one present was aware of the holy joy that filled her heart. When the bell announced the Solemn Act of the Mass, Teresita began her Act of Consecration to the Blessed Mother:

I, Teresa María Quevedo y Cadarso, a faithless sinner, renew and ratify today in thy hands, O Immaculate Mother, the vows of my Baptism; I renounce forever Satan, his pomps and works; and I give myself entirely to Jesus Christ, the Incarnate Wisdom, to carry my cross after Him all the days of my life, and to be more faithful to Him than I have ever been before.

In the presence of all the heavenly Court I choose thee this day for my Mother and Mistress. I deliver and consecrate to thee, as thy slave, my body and soul, my goods, both interior and exterior, and even the value of all my good actions, past, present and future; leaving to thee the entire and full right of disposing of me and all that belongs to me, without exception, according to thy good pleasure, for the greater glory of God, in time and in eternity. Amen.

The Sisters at Our Lady of Mount Carmel Academy were planning the reorganization of their *Congregante Mariana* (Sodality of the Blessed Virgin) in 1944. Mother Superior posted an edict stating that the sodalists-elect would have to be "the cream of the crop." The girls accepted the challenge enthusiastically and the Sisters were pleased to see improvement in every phase of student life, especially in conduct. In the spiritual realm, self-sacrifice and prayer permeated the very air.

On November fourth, a tribunal of teachers met to elect the students worthy of probationship. After a year, if they remained on the worthy list, these probationers would be received into the Sodality as permanent members.

Before the election took place, Teresita Quevedo wrote the following letter to the Blessed Virgin:

Most pure and immaculate Virgin Mary, Mother of God and my Mother: I, your unworthy child María Teresa Quevedo, want to thank you with all my heart for the many favors received through your intercession. My great desire and request today is that you may find me worthy of membership in your Sodality. If I am not, dear Blessed Lady, grant that I may always be a faithful child of yours outside the Sodality.

I have a strong desire to serve you, dear Lady! Now, in the presence of your Divine Son Jesus and of all the Heavenly Court, I promise what our retreat master suggested, "to defend the cause of Christ every day of my life; to live as a true child of Mary; to conquer human respect; to dress in conformity with the rule of Christian modesty; and never to attend or take part in any function that may in the least depreciate Catholic morals or Christian charity."

Most holy Mother of God, receive this humble offering from the hands of my holy patron, Saint Agnes, whom I have asked to present it to you. I beg you to mother me as your weakest child, to guide my every step, to defend me from my enemies, and to help me fulfill God's will every day of my life. Since your Divine Son has given me the grace to offer you this oblation, will you, dear Mother, give me the love and courage I need to carry it out.

María Teresa Quevedo.

Four days later, the names of Teresita and Carmen Quevedo were on the list of aspirants-elect that was posted on the bulletin board. There is no expression of Teresita's reaction to her pending membership in the Sodality. Impressions of onlookers, however, hint at the workings of grace in her soul during the months she prepared for her Child-of-Mary role. One of her associates said: "If the Sodality is only for *Angels,* who will bring to it less of the world than our Teresita?"

Several times during the course of that year, the Mother Superior of the Academy made remarks to Doctor Quevedo, such as: "Of late, when Teresita leaves the altar rail after receiving Holy Communion, Calixto, I cannot take my eyes from her, for grace seems to emanate from her gentle person."

Teresita's sister Carmen noticed the same thing as Reverend Mother. The girl once said to Sister Teresa: "Tere is not an ordinary little girl. If you aren't convinced of that, Sister, watch her when she comes from Holy Communion. She is angelic! Many of the girls have commented on her piety; older people, too, who see her at Mass with Papa occasionally."

A friend of Teresita, Mercedes Martin, told Sister Mary Teresa also that she needed no other proof to convince her of Teresita's holiness than to see her after she had received Communion. "Her face is an image of the happiness of the blessed," she said.

Another of Teresita's friends, Mercedes Aguirre, mentioned that: "Teresita was unusually absorbed in prayer in chapel. I loved to watch her praying to Our Lady. She always looked up so affectionately at the Blessed Virgin! I am sure she was begging her to make her a saint, for that is the only thing Teresita wanted."

Among Teresita's natural gifts we must include piety. "She was born with it," says one of her teachers. As a result of it, she was elected President of the Sodality of Our Lady.

The day after that election Teresita's piety led her to ask a unique favor of her parents. "Papa," she said at dinner, "Elsa Moreno is going to make a retreat at the Handmaids of the Sacred Heart Academy this weekend."

"Is she, dear?" What can she be leading up to? Don Calixto wondered.

"It is a special retreat for young girls, Papa, and I thought it would help me with my Sodality work if. . . ."

"The answer is *no,* Teresita," he broke in. Then, regretting his sharpness, he added: "You have made one retreat this year, Princess. You are too little for so much prayer. It is strenuous."

"Oh, Papa, don't you know that the smaller we are, the more we have to depend on Our Lady? Please, Papa! She will send you any favor you want if you let me make this retreat."

Doctor Quevedo gave in, as he always did when Teresita coaxed him.

On Friday, February first, he drove his "Princess" to the Handmaids' Academy on Martinez Campos Street. When he returned he said to his wife, "I don't know why I left her there, she is only a child. There are many Religious who don't make two retreats in one year. It isn't right. . . ."

"Yes it is, Calixto. Our Lady will take care of her." Doña María del Carmen was emphatic.

What kind of retreat notes did Teresita keep? Here they are:

SPIRITUAL EXERCISES. ACADEMY OF THE HANDMAIDS.

Since I have to think a great deal about the Sodality during these days, my writing will be brief, dear Lady.

My dear Mother Mary, please ask Jesus to give me the grace I need to make a good retreat; the light I need to know what kind of Sodality leader you want me to be, and the strength I need to be it.

Feb. 1. A.M.

We are made by God for Himself. What a terrible thing it would be to use God's own creations to offend Him!

Feb. 1. P.M.

To reach Heaven I must walk along a narrow road—a road of mortification and suffering. Mary, my Mother, take my hand. Lead me along the narrow path.

Feb. 2. A.M.

Jesus, beloved of my soul, let me die before I offend You. How good it is to be in retreat on my Mother's Purification feast! I love you, Sweet Lady!

Feb. 2. P.M.

Purity is my ermine cloak. Charity is my diamond crown. Mary is my Queen. Jesus is my King. I am a princess—a princess who is a slave to the Queen.

Feb. 3

My life must be with Christ, in Christ, for Christ—with Our Lady at my side.

Resolutions:
1. To meditate with Our Lady fifteen minutes every day.
2. Not to waste time. (It belongs to Jesus.)
3. To obey perfectly.

Teresita Quevedo

Teresita had her Sodality schedule well lined up when she returned to school the following Monday morning. "Weekly meetings will be necessary if we want the probationers to absorb the meaning of the Marian ideal, Padre. And I realize that I must not only encourage them but show them how to practice a lively love for Our Lady," she said to Father Antonio Martínez, S.J., Sodality adviser.

"You have established yourself as a natural leader, Teresita," he told her. Father was impressed not only by her own personal piety but by her genuine interest in that of the girls.

The day for selecting Marian mottoes arrived. They would be engraved on the medals the girls were to receive at the Sodality reception. It was an important moment! Each girl wrote her choice on an index card, signed her name, and dropped the card on Sister Teresa's desk. Father Martínez and Sister Teresa checked the mottoes later in the day.

"All for Jesus through Mary," was chosen by one of

Grignon de Montfort's devotees. "Compassionate Mother Mary, be my Salvation," was another. "Mary Most Pure, Guard my Purity," a third, and so on. Finally they came to Teresita's. She had chosen a motto that was not only an expression of her love for Our Lady, but also of her aim in life. It was: "My Mother, grant that everyone who looks at me may see you!"

First rule of the Sodality of Our Lady: "As many as are gathered under this title of Our Lady must be true Christians who sincerely strive for sanctification in their own respective state of life, and who work with earnest determination, as far as their social condition permits, to save and sanctify souls."

Few of the Sodalists took the twofold command of self-sanctification and one's neighbor's sanctification as deeply to heart as Teresita. It gave rise to a change in the new Sodality President. She became more receptive to grace, which gradually snuffed out childish defects. A sister Sodalist sums it up well when she says: "Teresita did not know mediocrity. When she made up her mind to submit to the workings of divine grace, she did it completely and forever."

One facet of the Blessed Virgin's Sodality in Spain is the Apostolate of the Poor. Soon after their reception into the Sodality, new Sodalists are introduced to the two phases of apostolic work which they are expected to carry on. One, the visitation of homes for the aged, run by the Little Sisters of the Poor. The other, catechizing poor children in the lower sections of Madrid.

The old folks at Saint Gabriel's Home in the center of the city used to anticipate the Sodalists' weekly visit with the joy of children. It was a moment to exchange the woes of age for the gaiety of youth. They reveled in the songs, dances, plays, even in the sweets Our Lady's troubadours offered them. Teresita, the youngest of the group, was one of the most tireless entertainers. A letter she wrote to Father Martínez will tell us why:

Dear Padre, you are right! The Apostolate is imperative if I want to be what God wishes me to be. So often these days I recall how you have repeated those words of Holy Scripture which tell us that on the day of judgment God will say to us: "Come, blessed of My Father, because I was thirsty, you gave Me to drink." Since this is true, we are bound to do good works. Whatever I do for the poor, I know I am doing for God. I try to see God in them. Frequently, working with them repulses me, Padre, but I shall always mortify myself so as not to fail in charity. God bless you....

Every Sunday morning the children from the poor parish of Saint Christina gathered in Saint Francis' Plaza for religious instruction. Teresita was there as a catechist. She believed herself less useful in this role than in that of comforter to the aged. Perhaps it was because her youth prevented her being assigned to a group of children. She was given the care of one little boy, Pepe. He was the son of a poor woman, a spiritualist, who held nightly sessions in her home. Pepe confided in Teresita from the start, and it was not long before he told her how his mother and her friends learned many "truths" from the spirits.

"Look, *hombrecito,*" said Tere, when she knew she had won his confidence, "you must not go to those sessions any more because ... well ... it is a sin."

"Dios mio, how can it be a sin if Mama does it?" he asked.

"Now I know that your mama is good, Pepe, but let's say that she is ... that she is mistaken," Tere explained.

The little ragamuffin seemed to understand that his mother

could make a mistake even if she did not sin. That saved the day!

Teresita then began to deny herself candy through the week, and every Sunday she would bring a generous bag of goodies to Pepe. She offered that denial to Our Lady for Pepe's complete surrender to grace.

Pepe, nevertheless, was worried. He could not tell his mother about her mistake. Just how could he get out of going to the "sessions?" After some hard thinking, he decided that there was a way. He could skip those sessions if he could get to bed early enough! So, for love of Mary, the little fellow changed the pattern of his life. He pretended to be exhausted every evening after supper, and it worked! His mother tucked him in bed before the meeting gathered at her home. "Poor Pepe is growing; he gets so terribly tired these days," she told her friends.

Teresita told Carmen some months after she had taken over her little charge, "I am very happy about Pepe. He is developing into a strong boy, mentally and physically. He prays sincerely and he loves the Blessed Virgin."

It was Teresita's privilege to prepare Pepe for his First Communion. She did so with an ardor that must have pleased God. The day before he was to receive Our Lord, Sister Teresa found Teresita kneeling before the Blessed Sacrament, her arms stretched out in the form of a cross. Sister watched the stiff figure for longer than she herself could have endured such a posture. Fearing the child might exhaust herself to the point of fainting, Sister tapped her lightly on the shoulder and said: "Tere, why pray in this position so long?" The large blue eyes were raised to her beloved aunt as she responded: "Tía, Pepe at this moment is about to make his First Confession and I want him to do it well. I am asking Our Lady to give him a grace that will keep him climbing the ladder of holiness."

The last Sunday of October, 1943, was but a few days off . . . Feast of Christ the King and Mission Sunday. The Carmelites of Charity had organized a rally to celebrate the twenty-fifth anniversary of the "Youth for Missions" groups. It was to be held in Tarragona, where more than four hundred representatives from the Carmelite of Charity Schools, hospitals and orphanages would gather to honor all fields of missionary work. Dozens of other religious communities would send groups to join them.

For weeks the students at the Academy in Saint Francis' Plaza in Madrid had been practicing the mission song which begins:

> Souls, souls was the glorious cry
> Echoed when Youth for Missions was formed.
> Souls, souls, in a gesture of love,
> Are offered to Christ on the Cross.

It was a time of suspense . . . of sacrifice and prayer. Suspense, because everyone wondered which girls would be selected to make up the body of representatives from Madrid. Moreover, one girl would be chosen Standard Bearer, an honor every student wanted.

Sacrifice comprised the mission activity of the month. Customarily, each girl sacrificed this or that luxury in order to put aside pesetas for the final mission collection. And besides her own prayer-filled offerings, she solicited whatever spiritual aid available from generous relatives and friends.

Father Martínez tells us that: "Teresita Quevedo, rallying all her physical and moral forces, worked like a little slave, gathering money, stamps and prayers for the missions. She denied herself the luxuries a girl of her age ordinarily enjoyed, saving her pesetas for the missions. That particular year, of her own savings, she gave 1,633 pesetas (about $63.00 at that time) to the mission collection. Tremendous sacrifice on the part of a thirteen-year-old girl!"

Emotion was at its peak when Reverend Mother rose before the student body in the auditorium on Friday morning to announce the names of the "chosen ones." It wasn't an unusually long list, but the suspense that filled the room made it seem so. Mother finished reading the roster. Then, picking up a piece of paper from the table, she read: "Because of her outstanding work for the missions during the month of October, 1943, Teresa María Quevedo has been selected by the faculty to act as Standard Bearer for the representatives from Madrid."

A thunderous applause swallowed up the meek *"Gracias, Madre"* that Teresita proffered.

It was a glorious rally, they tell us. There was a Solemn High Mass at noon and one of Spain's eminent Jesuits delivered the sermon. His text was taken from the writings of a one-time Papal Nuncio to the Royal Court of Italy, Cardinal Borgongini-Duca. Quoting the Cardinal, Father said:

> ... The missionary priests and Sisters have sacrificed everything for the love of God. All that men and women hold dear—life, loved ones and country—have been cheerfully given up by them to carry the Gospel of Christ to pagan lands.
>
> We should pray that God may increase the number of these heroes, and even though it may not be our privilege to be numbered among these valiant soldiers of Christ we may still have a share in the glorious work which they are doing. We should not allow them to think that we have abandoned them in the

trying struggle which they are making against overwhelming difficulties. We should encourage them by our prayers, and, if it is possible, by our offerings. We should read the periodicals which tell of missionary life, missionary activities, and missionary hardships and heartbreaks. We should be Apostles of Good with at least the same zeal and interest with which the wicked propagate evil. For every effort, for every sacrifice, which we make for the children of Christ as yet outside the Church of Christ, we shall receive a hundredfold return. And if we are the means of bringing even one soul to the knowledge and love of God, our reward is great in heaven.

Teresita's reaction to that inspiring sermon is found in her confessor's words: "She wanted to be an Apostle of Good. A few months after the rally she sent a generous gift of pesetas to Alaska to Father Llorente, S.J., a classmate of her uncle Antonio. She asked him to make her the godmother of a little Alaskan girl. . . ."

The grateful Jesuit wrote her the following letter:

My dear Teresita, A thousand thanks for your letter which I enjoyed very much. Enclosed I am sending you a photograph of your little godchild whom I have baptized Maria Teresa Klujnalpk. Pray that she may join you in Heaven some day. She is a very sweet little girl and will make her First Communion on Christmas Eve.

I know your Uncle Antonio very well; we studied together in the seminary and later on were stationed together in Cuba. . . . Pray for us and we will pray for you and for all your family. With a blessing,

Your missionary friend from Alaska,
Segundo Llorente, S.J.

Teresita loved the picture of her namesake and continued to save and to beg money and stamps for Father Llorente's Eskimo mission. She enclosed her last donations in a letter in which she told Father about her desire to become a Religious. "I have only one fear," she concluded, "and I beg you to pray, Padre, that if I should become a Religious I will be a good one, for the thought of being a mediocre Religious terrifies me."

CHAPTER V

A Vow

ONE October morning in 1945, Sister Teresa was at her desk checking Sodality files, when Teresita walked into her office. She greeted her aunt and, going straight to the heart of the matter, asked: "Tía Teresa, can you recommend a good confessor? I prefer a Jesuit—someone I can contact soon. I have a few problems, one in particular, that need attention."

Sister Teresa immediately telephoned Father Joaquín Muzquiz, S.J., and asked him if he would see her niece. Father had known the Quevedo family through Teresita's Jesuit uncles and he was eager to lend an interested ear to her needs. That is how Teresita happened to meet the wise Jesuit who counseled her until Our Lady placed her soul in the hands of her Divine Director.

After his first meeting with Teresita, Father Muzquiz said that "she was favored with very special grace from God." He found "her constant striving for perfection extremely rare in a girl of her age." To which he added: "Humble and good as Teresita was, I did not understand the quality of her virtue until I became aware of her devotion to Our Lady. It was clear then why God favored her—Mary was her life."

Father Muzquiz frequently spoke to Sodality groups on the "Love of Mary in the Modern World." After he met Teresita Quevedo, his talks were "brightened and strengthened" with concrete examples of how a Child of Mary can love God and also love the world in which she lives. "I found a unique combination of holiness and gaiety in Teresita," Father wrote. "She enjoyed everything. Her interest in art, music and poetry was lively and normal. Teresita was an enthusiast for parties and an ardent sportswoman. In fact, she sympathized with the whole world—the good world. Her love for her family, relatives and friends was strong. All of God's creations were precious to her, but she was careful not to let love for any one of them rob God of an atom of her love for Him. Indeed, I felt obliged to use this knowledge of a modern girl and of her way of using all things for God's glory as a means to help other sodalists along a path of love."

It was an Indian Summer afternoon in 1945. Teresita Quevedo rang the bell of Father Muzquiz's office, which was located on the Paseo de La Castellana in Madrid. Sitting opposite Father's large mahogany desk, Teresita felt lost in a huge red leather chair. "There are so many things in life that remind us of our littleness, Padre," she began. "This chair, for example." Her laughter was as genuine as the tinkle of antique crystal.

"It serves its purpose, then, Teresita," Father smiled. "I always say that if a poor Jesuit must have luxury in his office, let it serve some good purpose. Today, it incites humility; tomorrow, another virtue. I hope my friends carry those pious experiences away with them. . . ."

Teresita, usually ready for light banter with Father, was not given to it on that particular afternoon. She quickly reached the point of her visit.

"Padre, something of importance brings me here this afternoon—something I've been praying over for more than a year. I am confident that the time has come to act. . . ." She paused.

"Yes, Teresita?" Father felt that she had come to discuss a religious vocation.

But she hadn't. "I would like to make a vow of purity to Our Lord, Padre," she said with equanimity.

"A vow of purity?" Father Muzquiz questioned.

"Yes, Padre. I am fifteen years old. Our Lady's Virginity inspires me to give my purity to Christ now. I think I should follow the inspiration, Padre."

"That is a wonderful grace, my child. How jealously you guard your purity! That is pleasing to the Heart of Christ." Father was moved by her candor and wisdom.

"But first, Padre, I would like to make a General Confession."

"Of course, Teresita. We shall talk at length about your pending vow in the confessional."

"The above conversation took place on the feast of the Presentation, November twenty-first," Father Muzquiz tells us. "On the feast of Our Lady's Immaculate Conception, in the Presence of the Blessed Sacrament in the Academy chapel, Teresita Quevedo solemnly vowed the purity of her body and soul to God."

Before she knelt to say her night prayers on that memorable feast, Teresita opened her missal and wrote on a picture of Our Lady that she always kept there to mark the December eighth Mass:

Most Holy Mother:

Today I have solemnly promised
to live holy and chaste forever.
My only desire is to give You,
Jesus and Mary, pure pleasure.

Teresita and Carmen studied French with the Notre Dame Sisters at Holy Cross Academy, not far from their home. Mère Marie, the Mother Superior, had a wide reputation for holiness. It was rumored in Madrid that high Church dignitaries went to her for counsel. The Quevedo girls seldom met Mère Marie during their years of study at Holy Cross. When they did, she would stop to check up on their progress by chatting with them in French. Mère Marie revered their father, physician to the community at Holy Cross, which explains the kindly interest she took in his daughters.

On Holy Saturday afternoon in 1946, Carmen and Teresita stopped at Holy Cross to wish their French teachers a Happy Easter. Mère Marie happened along. Delighted to see the girls, she visited with them in the parlor.

"Mère Marie was very jovial and chatty," Carmen told her mother later, "but she never took her eyes from Tere's face until we were leaving. I was glad she didn't look through me like that, Mama!"

Teresita had been unaware of Mère Marie's scrutinizing gaze. In fact, she had enjoyed their conversation. However, she did become a bit disconcerted, she tells us, when Mère Marie put her hand on her head as they were leaving and said to Carmen: "This little one has a big secret in her heart."

Only Father Muzquiz knew her secret!

Carmen had not thought twice about Mère Marie's remark. She knew nothing of her sister's vow of purity. Yet she did see a new Teresita, for she mentioned as much in this letter she wrote to her friend Cristina. . . .

Dear Cristina: Too bad you weren't in Madrid to celebrate Tere's sixteenth birthday! Mama and Papa gave her a wonderful party. . . . She looks quite the same to me as she did a year ago—no taller—but she seems older. I'm not sure that older is what I mean, Cristina; perhaps I should say she seems *different*. She is far more attractive than I, much livelier, but completely disinterested in boys. That's where she is different! Most of our girl friends have a few heart interests. Not Tere—she doesn't care a hoot about romance. I am annoyed with her. . . .

Oscar and I were discussing Tere at the party. Among other things, he said to me: "What a girl Tere is! She overflows with charm; she is popular, but she won't give one of the fellows a 'break.' "

He went on to tell me that most of the boys think Tere is "a doll." They admire and respect her, but they find something "hard-to-define about her." I don't know why she is so aloof. Oscar and I intend to talk to her about it. . . .

The aloofness, to which Carmen refers, was not only her natural modesty but also an expression of Teresita's undivided love for Christ. And Our Blessed Mother—the love of Teresita's life—shielded her from any human love that sought absolute response in her affections. Teresita Quevedo was merely fulfilling her pledge to Mary when she held her reserve with the young Spanish caballeros. But how would Carmen and Oscar know that! How could they understand that while they enjoyed the pleasures of youth, Teresita gave her soul to the divine pleasure of God!

Certainly youth could not be expected to penetrate a haze that clouded the understanding of a person as mature as Doña María del Carmen Quevedo. For neither was she able to interpret Teresita's lack of interest in the several friends of Luis—good boys with mental and physical attractions—whose attentions toward her would have been lavish had she given them an ounce of encouragement. Doña María grew disturbed about it during the year following Tere's sixteenth birthday party, for she believed that every young girl should not only desire the gallantries of a suitor, but should reassure him if she were fortunate enough to have one. However, Teresita was still young, her mother thought, and perhaps by the time she reached her eighteenth birthday she would show some interest in boys. (In Spain it is not customary for a young lady of Teresita's social class to go out alone with a boy or to dance with boys before her eighteenth birthday. For that reason, most girls' parents have them trained early in folk-dancing, which satisfies their yen to "trip the light fantastic" until they make their debut.)

The girls attended a host of parties during the 1946-47 season. They were either celebrations for Teresita's seventeen-year-old friends or debuts for classmates of Carmen. "The girls returned from each party buoyant . . . bubbling with descriptions of gowns and appraisals of new acquaintances . . . ," Mrs. Quevedo relates. "I always studied Tere well, hoping to find a new sparkle in her eye. I should have known better, for the ever-cheerful humor and innocence that she radiated would have far outshone a human heart interest—I realized that too late. However, the days immediately following a party would reveal the fulfillment of my hope, I used to tell myself. But it was ever the same—phone calls, several a day, came from boys the girls had met at those parties. Not one of the calls was for Teresita. It troubled me greatly and I decided to speak to her about it.

" 'Tere,' I said one morning when we were alone at breakfast, 'Carmen seems to be very popular with the boys. Why is it they never call you on the phone?'

" 'Because, Mama, they know I do not want them to call me.'

"I could not pursue the question further because the beauty of truth flooded her face."

One final word on Teresita's party days from her loyal friend Cristina Parrella: "The fact that Teresita had no involvements in petty love—as the rest of us so often did—does not mean that she was prudish. She was farther removed from that than any of us. Tere was what the Sisters at the Academy advised all of us to be until we had made our debut—utterly 'general' when boys came into the picture. That was the secret of her popularity, I believe. Everyone flocked around Tere at a party, especially the boys, because her repartee was sparkling. She also had a remarkable talent for remembering witty stories and had a veritable treasure chest of riddles which she would unearth whenever a lull punctuated the evening's mirth. . . . Tere loved people. And she loved parties—I never knew her to miss one."

Teresita's irrepressible spirit was not hampered by her "secret." Letters from Fuenterrabia to her friends in Madrid, the following summer, show a gaiety of heart typical of her. In June she wrote to Angelines:

Dearest Cousin, We came here this year on the express train—Tía Josefina, Carmen and I. It was not crowded, and Tía dozed most of the way. Carmen and I were fascinated by a married couple who were going to San Sebastian on their honeymoon. Not the first one either! Many years ago, their conversation told us, he had been there as a bridegroom for the first time. We couldn't tell about her. However, he had lost his youth and resembled one of those pictures of the lean Renaissance poets in our literature texts. No matter, he treated her very courtly. Nothing he could do to increase her comfort was too much. When we stopped to take passengers on at Burgos, he almost carried her to the observation car to get a glimpse of Miraflores.* At that point, Carmen and I started to giggle and wakened Tía Josefina. It struck us so funny, Nines, to see the bride towering head and shoulders over her husband, as they walked down the aisle of the car.

We haven't been here a week and we've had a revolting experience. I wouldn't relate it, Nines, except that I believe it may help to prevent you from a similar eventuality. The Vinuesas took the members of our Tennis Club to France on their motor boat. We wore bathing suits and the sun gave us a tan you would envy.

We reached the beach at Sainte Jeanne de Luz early in the afternoon. Mr. Vinuesas told us to hop ashore and join our French neighbors in a swim. Carmen and I leaped like kangaroos, we were so anxious to chat with them in French. However, we stopped dead in our tracks before we reached them. Nines, I cannot tell you how disgusted we were—surrounded by a vulgar array of Bikinis. It spoiled what might have been a perfect afternoon. Believe me, there wasn't a protest when Mrs. Vinuesas rang the deck bell which announced the time for our return to Fuenterrabia.

On the trip back to Spain, Mr. Vinuesas remarked that the "Frenchies" looked at us as if we were a species of rare beings from antiquity. I can not help but wonder how Our Lady feels about such immodest dress. If we turn our eyes away, what must she do? I hope our Mother of Purity finds some comfort in her old-fashioned Spaniards, Nines!

The novena to Our Lady of Guadalupe begins tomorrow. Since she is the patroness of this town, everyone will make it.

I am playing good tennis, Nines, so I warn you . . . you had better get in trim for the September matches!

* Carthusian Monastery renowned for its architectural elegance.

Mama is calling me to get dressed for Rosa Moliner's birthday party. Adiós, Nines, write me soon, and don't forget our pact to say a Rosary daily!

My love to you and the family,

Tere.

Our Lady must have been pleased with her Spanish children's reaction to that trip to Sainte Jeanne de Luz. Teresita's aunts have since wondered if it acted as a catalyst in forming their niece's decision to enter the convent.

Shortly after her experience at the French resort, Teresita spoke of a vocation in a letter to Father Muzquiz. On the eve of the feast of Our Lady of Mount Carmel (1946) she wrote: "I have seen God's will very clearly—He wants me to become a Religious. . . ."

That was the first and last mention Teresita made of her vocation until Father, taking the initiative on the feast of the Ascension in 1947, asked her if she still saw God's will regarding her future life as she had seen it on July 16, 1946.

"Yes, Padre. I plan to enter the convent," she replied. "I know God wills that. My desires are much stronger now than they were a year ago. In fact, Padre, I would like to enter this year, if you find no reason to advise otherwise."

Father asked her what Community of Sisters she planned to enter. Teresita answered without hesitation: "The Carmelites of Charity, Padre. They have been my teachers for twelve years. Besides, Papa has four sisters in the Institute. But I have chosen the Institute principally because it is a Congregation which has as its end the glorification of the Blessed Virgin."

"Teresita's vocation from then on was clear to me," Father Muzquiz writes. "As the weeks lengthened into months, I could detect a passion to please God in all that she did. She remained calm and serene exteriorly, however, and no one would have suspected the plan she held in her heart. The fidelity she showed to God through her prayers and mortifications during the months before she entered the convent was edifying. . . ."

Teresita Quevedo's humility guarded her from being absolutely sure of anything but God's love, and of anyone but God and Our Lady. Therefore, regarding her entrance into the convent, she did not entertain hopeful thoughts that would be natural to a young girl whose grandmother had given four daughters to the Institute of the Carmelite Sisters of Charity. Neither did it dawn on Teresita that she might be accepted into that Congregation more readily because of the widespread reputation for holiness of her scholarly uncle, Antonio Quevedo, S.J. Nor did it occur to her to solicit the aid of one of Spain's outstanding retreat masters, her second Jesuit uncle, Jesús Quevedo. The question of her vocation was something to be resolved between God and herself—through the direction of her confessor and the decision of the superiors at Carabanchel, the Carmelite Provincial House.

Lest she might be denied admittance, Teresita decided it would be well to petition the Mother Superior for entrance to the novitiate before disclosing her secret to the family or to her Jesuit uncles and Carmelite aunts. Father Muzquiz sanctioned her proposal and made the arrangements for Teresita to call at the Provincial House of the Carmelites of Charity to talk to the Mother General, who was in Madrid at the time.

Tere was presented to the Reverend Mother General by Mother María Teresa Rodriguez, the religious superior of Our Lady of Mount Carmel Academy. Mother General warmly greeted the girl whose family she had known for years, and invited her to have a seat.

With no preamble whatever, but with utter simplicity, Teresita told the Reverend Mother: "I would like to become a Carmelite of Charity if you will receive me into the Institute, Mother."

After a number of pertinent questions, Mother General indicated that it would be her pleasure, for there seemed to be no impediments to prevent her from doing so. Teresita enjoyed a fine reputation at Our Lady of Mount Carmel Academy, she came from the best of families and seemed to have the qualifications necessary to embrace the life of a Carmelite Sister of Charity.

There was the slightest pause and Teresita made immediate use of it to suggest: "I would like to enter in February, if I may, Reverend Mother."

"That, my dear, will depend on your father's decision, for you are not eighteen years old—nor will you be in February. If he agrees to your wish, Teresita, I am sure the council will be happy to receive you in February," the wise Mother General stated.

"And then, Reverend Mother," Teresita continued, "may I go to the mission in China?"

Mother answered her smiling: "We shall see, Teresita. But to the novitiate first, my dear." She was amused at the speed with which this young girl wanted to propel herself to the Orient.

Teresita's propensity for accelerated motion was not always rewarded with a smile, as it had been by the amused Mother General. At times, it was rebuked by her father with a stern frown. Doctor Quevedo tells us that when it came to automobiles Teresita was the best driver among his children, but she traveled at a daring speed. "Frequently I had to restrict her use of the car, only because I feared that her speed would lead to danger," he relates. "She was, nevertheless, as careful as a fast driver can be on the road; she handled the car well, and she never violated the law. But when she set out with a fixed destination, for some unknown reason she had to get there quickly. My only comfort was her devotion to Our Lady, for whenever I cautioned her about speeding she would reply: 'Don't worry, Papa; you know Our Blessed Lady rides with me.' And I believe the Mother of God did keep my winged child from harm."

We shall note below that the urge "to speed" had permeated the activities of Teresita's life long before she was old enough to drive a car.

"Your daughter Teresita is a remarkable swimmer, Doctor Quevedo," one of the lifeguards at the Nautical Club observed as they watched the young people enjoying the water on a very warm Summer afternoon.

"Indeed! She glides through the water with an ease that electrifies me," added an old friend who sat beside the doctor. "Did you teach her to swim, Calixto?"

"Let me say I began to teach her to swim—when she was six years old," Doctor Quevedo replied with a twinkle in his eye. "But before many seasons had passed, Tere found my method too slow and she set out on her own. Now she outswims every member of the family."

"Does she dive?" the lifeguard inquired with a hopeful expression on his face. He might have another entry for the high-diving contest!

"Does she! Like a mermaid. But you will have to take her out in a boat with a springboard to see her do it. That is Teresita's specialty. However, if you have in mind what I suspect, Juan, I do not encourage you to approach her, for she declined Don Rafael's invitation to take part in the diving contests."

The lifeguard could not understand why a modern, pretty

and charming girl, so expert in the water, would have no interest in amassing medals that she could win with ease. If he could influence her to enter the contest it would be a feather in his cap, for he knew now that she had refused Don Rafael, the manager of the Club. "She is human," he thought, as he sprinted along the sandy beach. "I'm sure I can convince her to sign up. Never met a girl yet that refused me!" As he neared a group of girls that were coming out of the water, he threw out his brawny chest, raised his handsome head, and walked toward them.

"*Hola,* girls," he smiled.

"*Hola,* Juan," they smiled in return and stopped, perhaps flattered by his gracious attention. Tere, however, continued on toward the lockers. She had walked a few yards before she realized that she was being followed.

"May I speak with you for a minute?" Juan asked as he overtook Teresita. "I presume you are in a hurry and I will not detain you, Miss Quevedo." He flashed what would ordinarily be a disarming smile.

"No, I am not in a hurry," Tere replied, unconsciously deflating Juan's ego.

He explained the reason for his approach to her, but Tere would not consider his proposal. In answer to a question on whether she found diving a challenge, she replied: "Yes. I love to swim, of course, but I find nothing so thrilling as diving from a boat into the rolling waves of the sea."

"Why, then, won't you take part in our contests? From what your father tells me, Miss Quevedo, none of the participants in your age bracket can match your speed or your technique as a diver. (Teresita was sixteen at the time.) Think of the honor it will bestow on you! And of the glory it will bring to your father," he coaxed. Juan had a genuine admiration for Doctor Quevedo.

"Will it bring honor and glory to the Mother of God?" Tere asked Juan with the candor of a child.

Had Juan been as clever—or holy—as he was handsome, he might have won the desired candidate. But he was not. He was ill prepared for that question and his reply clinched Teresita's decision. "Oh, Miss Quevedo," he stammered, "well, let's leave her—I mean the Blessed Virgin—out of this."

"Bueno, Juan, if that is what you wish," she answered. "And I'll stay with Our Lady."

It is clear now that Teresita Quevedo had a more significant end in view than that of perfecting herself in a particular sport when she set out to acquire skill in it. What was the end that stimulated Teresita? And did "speed" really enter into it? Speed, as we know, is sometimes synonymous with recklessness, and speedy people are often heedless. Teresita could not be placed in either category, for she was not careless in any sense of the word and, paradoxically, she was known to do things in moderation. Actually, it was not her speed that attracted attention when she performed in the various sport activities. Sister Teresa has told us that "time and again the spectators who watched the interclass basketball games at the Academy gym would ask: 'Who is the blond girl that plays with all her might?" Even though other girls on the court were faster, better players, or higher scorers, something about Tere's intensity held the spectator's attention.

Intensity is the word. It was the way in which Teresita Quevedo "gave her all" to the game that impressed those who watched her play. Therefore, what has been referred to as speed in Tere's activities was not essentially speed. It was an intense self-giving—a complete thrusting of self into the project at hand, and a tireless effort to master it. That was Teresita's drive. That was her entire approach to life.

Mother Anita, one of Doctor Quevedo's older sisters, knew Teresita better probably than any of her relatives. Mother is the oldest of the four Carmelites of Charity, the aunt whom Tere saw least, but the one she loved best. Some people found their deep friendship incredible because of the difference in age and the distance that had always separated them. But it was genuine. Age need not enter here and souls are not the slaves of space. That friendship was but another of God's gifts to Teresita.

"Tere placed confidences in her dear Tía Anita that she shared with no one else," Sister Teresa tells us. "We know that whenever Mother Anita visited the Academy, Teresita begged a holiday because she wanted to be with her every possible minute.

"Alone in the garden—or wherever we happened to be—my dear little niece would bring up the topic of holiness," Mother Anita relates. "She always wanted to know how she could become holy more quickly. I would not be able to tell you how many, many times Teresita said to me, 'I am in a hurry to grow holy, Tía.' Among the few letters that I have kept through the years are those which Teresita wrote me from the Academy. Each one, strangely (perhaps not), ends with the same words: 'My only desire is to become holy, Tía, in order to please God and my beautiful Mother Mary. I will do whatever is necessary to become holy quickly.' Teresita did not mean 'quickly' in the usual sense of the word. What she meant was that she wanted every fiber of her being to work intensely and incessantly on the one project of her life—her sanctity."

CHAPTER VI

Vocation

A LIGHT frown puckered Teresita's face. Seated in the senior classroom one September afternoon beside her best friend, she asked: "Carmen, do you think it would be a disgrace for me to be graduated from school without having won a Badge of Honor?"

Teresita's ambitions, stimulated since she joined the Sodality, branched now into every phase of her life. Her desires to please the Blessed Virgin did not allow her a moment's rest. She must forever conquer something for love of Mary!

"Before I had time to answer her," said Carmen Aguado, "Tere continued: 'I have to win it, no matter what. I must win it.' "

Some months later, Reverend Mother posted the distribution of awards for the tri-semester of the 1947-1948 year. The list opened with: Senior Year Classical: Badge of Honor, Señorita María Teresa Quevedo y Cadarso.

That particular wish to show her love for Our Lady was satisfied.

The feast of the Presentation of the Blessed Virgin is impressively celebrated at the Academy of Our Lady of Mount Carmel. Prior to the forming of the procession on that feast day in 1947, Sister Teresa had given her usual lecture to the Sodality girls. She had told them how they should assist at the procession with deep Marian piety. The girls knew the talk by heart, nevertheless they enjoyed hearing it repeated year after year by their Prefect. The hour to form the procession arrived. The little girls in their best uniforms and white veils looked serious beyond their years; then followed the intermediates, that endless collection of jumping-jacks apparently transformed into a choir of angels. Finally the older girls—shall we call them the archangels of the lot? In the last group Teresita walked, singing with the rest: "This poor little soul surrenders her purity to Jesus through your hands, O María! O *Madre mia,* keep me pure in His sight! May He grant me forever His love and His light!"

As the Sister Prefect looked at Teresita with her cast-down eyes, her so-reverently joined hands, the nun sensed the supernatural about the girl. Teresita seemed completely absorbed in God and unaware of her external surroundings. It was then for the first time that Sister Teresa seriously wondered if her niece had a religious vocation. If God would not give one to her, to whom would He give one? she thought. Meanwhile the procession was entering the pews in chapel. All voices were raised in praise of Mary; but Teresita, as she knelt, burst into tears. This strange act, so contrary to the way of her light-hearted niece, did not escape Sister Teresa. What troubled her?

"Come in," called Sister Teresa in response to a knock on her office door.

"Buenas tardes, Tía, you sent for me?" asked the blue-eyed

blond who entered. "What a perfect day this has been, Tía, and what a pity that it will be my last Presentation procession!"

"A beautiful day indeed, Tere, but didn't it find you a bit sad? Why were you crying in chapel?"

A dozen legitimate excuses came to Teresita's mind and as she was deciding which one to use, her aunt continued, "*Bueno,* Tere, you don't have to tell me. I think I know. Isn't it because you think you have a religious vocation?"

That disarmed Teresita. She told her aunt that she *knew* she had a vocation and that she had resolved to follow it.

Delighted, but resuming the role of Sodality Prefect, Sister Teresa asked: "Why do you want to become a Religious, Teresita?"

"Because I believe that it is the path Christ wishes me to follow," she replied sincerely.

"Don't you love your family, your home and the world as you used to?"

"Oh yes, Tía," she replied firmly, "but I am willing to leave them all for God."

"And what Community do you intend to enter, Tere?"

"Oh Tía, what a question! Why, the Carmelites of Charity," she responded with respectful laughter.

"Good, my child, but think about it carefully, very carefully . . ." and before she had time to finish, Tere exclaimed:

"No, Tía. I have it all thought out. The semester will end in January and I plan to enter in February. I shall not tell the family, however, until after Christmas."

Sister Teresa was the astonished person now! But she did not hesitate to say, "No, Tere, no; you are too young. You should wait—as I did—until you are twenty years old."

"But I am willing, Tía, to enter at seventeen. Father Muzquiz approves of it," replied Tere. "I want to ask a favor of you now, Tía: please do not tell my secret because I want to be the first to tell Papa and Mama. I do not plan to tell them until the seventh of January so as not to upset their Christmas. In the meantime, Tía, will you let me spend an extra hour during the day on my embroidery, for I would like to finish the luncheon set for Mama before I enter the convent?"

Sister Teresa answered with a tight, wordless embrace and led her niece to the chapel where they both knelt in thanksgiving at the feet of Our Blessed Lady.

The following day, November 22, 1947, the Academy girls made their monthly day of recollection. After evening Benediction, Teresita confided to her religious notebook:

22 - XI - 47

To Jesus through Mary.

Resolutions:

To be more affectionate and self-sacrificing at home.

To say a Rosary every morning for my intention.

To give good example at school, particularly on line, at change of classes, at recreation and at sewing hour.

O most holy Virgin, help me to fulfill these resolutions and help me to be always good and pure. My Mother, I love you with all my heart. Today is Saturday—your day. Henceforth, I promise to write my regard for you as best I can, dear Blessed Virgin, every Saturday of the year. Perhaps I may need it sometime to hurdle the mountain of discouragement.

Teresita continued her normal life at the Academy, and it was no time until she faced the Christmas holidays. Just to think of the day when she would leave home made her heart skip a beat. Only outwardly did she remain calm; her "secret" vigorously shook the serenity of her heart.

One day after recreation during which, according to Carmen García, they had "played and laughed like clowns," the girls went into the washroom to tidy up before the next class. Teresita said to Carmen:

"Would you like to hear some big news? This is going to be my last semester at school, Carmen."

"Don't be silly!" answered Carmen. Then, realizing that Teresita was not joking, she asked in a weak voice, "You aren't going to be married, Tere, are you? Oh, tell me . . . this is terrible."

"Promise to keep it a secret?"

"I promise, I promise anything. . . ."

"Well . . . I am going to enter the novitiate," Tere announced.

It took a few minutes for Carmen to recover from that shock. She tried to express her emotions in words but failed. Then she buried her face in her hands and sobbed.

Teresita tried to comfort her; "Oh, Carmen, don't cry! . . . I am so happy! Look at me, Carmen! I am sure you are weeping only because you don't know what it means to belong to God."

"But, you can't go . . ." stammered Carmen. She could not imagine life at school without Teresita.

"Carmen, listen to me. God wants me to enter, so He will teach you to understand it in time. Right now I need your help. I need your prayers so that my family may not try to stop me. I am going to tell them my plans on January seventh. Please pray for me, Carmen, and for them, too. The only pain I shall feel is the parting from my family and the relinquishing of my Sodality medal."

"Your medal, Tere? Can't you take it with you?"

"No, Carmen." And with the naturalness so characteristic of Teresita, she took a beribboned medal from her coat pocket. For a moment she let it dangle, admiring it. Then she pulled the blue satin ribbon over Carmen's head and said: "There, my friend, is Teresita's proudest possession. Keep it forever, and may it keep you!"

Christmas! A word which for twenty centuries has spelled *joy, peace, love* and *giving*. Giving . . . that was what worried Teresita. A paradox, she thought. Certainly she was giving to God, but how would her family look upon it? Would they consider it taking from them?

It was the first Christmas that Teresita ever knew the anxieties of a divided heart as she took part in the season's festivities. Everything she desired, everything she hoped for seemed to lurk in the shadow of *adiós,* of an *adiós* that she had never before experienced.

The seventh of January arrived at last! It was Wednesday, and Teresita went to early Mass so that she could go to Confession first. Teresita came from the Sacrament filled with a new confidence in God. When Father Muzquiz asked her if she felt nervous about breaking the news to her family, she answered a decided *no*. "I must say," Father Muzquiz tells us, "that Teresita's unalterable peace, in perhaps the most painful moment that one who has a religious vocation has to endure, made a remarkable impression on me."

Teresita's father always took the customary siesta after meals. So, after the midday meal on January seventh, Don Calixto went to his room. But he had scarcely put his head on the pillow when Teresita softly opened his bedroom door and whispered:

"Papa, are you asleep?"

"No, come in. Do you want something, Princess?"

"Yes, Papa, but if you want to sleep, I'll come back later."

"Come in, dear, come in," repeated Mr. Quevedo.

Teresita timidly approached her father. She knelt on his bed and, looking affectionately at him, said with a little catch in her voice: "Papa, I dread saying this to you, because it is going to hurt you, but . . ." (Somehow Don Calixto guessed all that his daughter had come to tell him.)

"Go on, Princess, tell me. What is it you want?"

"I want to become a Carmelite," she replied firmly.

Her father relates that even though he had been expecting it, when the actual moment came, it was a shock.

"Teresita," her father asked, "do you realize what that means? You have always been so full of life—so fond of sports . . . dancing . . . and parties . . . ," he broke off.

"Yes, but none of that *satisfies* me, Papa."

"My dear child, do you know that to become a Religious means to lead a life of sacrifice?"

"Yes, Papa, I know it. That is why I want to enter the convent.

"Does your confessor know anything about this?" Don Calixto's question was asked hopefully. Perhaps he believed her confessor could hold her off for a few years.

"Yes, Papa, he knows it and he thinks that I have a true vocation."

"And when do you want to enter?" he asked with resignation in his voice, for his hope was shattered.

"Well, Papa, I would like to enter in February."

Not a word of contradiction. Not a negation. None of the reasonable protests which involuntarily arise from affection and love. He simply said: "Well, let's call Mama and tell her, Princess."

"No, Papa, not yet. Mama is getting dressed for one of those concerts she enjoys so much. If we tell her, she will not go."

Don Calixto shook his head. He must call his wife immediately.

To Mrs. Quevedo the news was a bitter blow. Teresita

told friends that it was the first time she had ever seen her mother cry. Carmen felt as her Mother did. Alone with Teresita later that day she said, "It doesn't seem right that you didn't even tell me. But I know why you kept your secret, Tere, you didn't want to spoil our Christmas."

Her secret known at home, Teresita wrote the following letter to her friend and former teacher:

Madrid, Jan. 12, 1948

To Jesus through Mary
Hermana Antonio Orozco: Dearest Sister, Thank you for your Christmas letter, which I loved very much. I do not know whether you have heard that I am not returning to the Academy in February, Sister. Instead, God willing, I am going to enter your novitiate. Did you expect this? I have not mentioned it because I did not like to entrust it to a letter. (You know how I hate to write anyway!) I have realized for some time that I have a vocation to the Carmelites of Charity but Father Muzquiz, who is my confessor, advised me not to tell anyone for a while. This didn't cost me anything because, as Tía Teresa says, I am naturally reserved and can keep a secret.

We spent the Christmas holidays very pleasantly because I did not tell Mama and Papa of my entrance until the day after the Epiphany. They are so good! They do not oppose me at all. Even though their hearts are aching, they act happy and eager to give their youngest child to God.

On January ninth I had to ask Reverend Mother's permission to enter the novitiate. She granted it provided Mama and Papa write her their consent. When I asked Papa if he would write Reverend Mother he said: "Of course; I cannot oppose a way of life that can lead only to Heaven."

Sister, I am filled with desires to be good. Do pray for me, for I need prayers now more than ever. Imagine, Tía Carmen will not only be my aunt now but also my mother. And she, the Mistress of Novices, was the last of the family to know!

I will have some photos taken soon and send them to you. Don't forget to pray for your child who loves you very much.

María Teresa.

Teresita was not the only one to break the news in a letter.

After consoling his wife, Doctor Quevedo went to his study, sat at the desk, opened his tooled leather writing pad and picked up an American fountain pen. Twirling it between his fingers he said to Daria who was drawing the curtains against the evening dusk: "It has been so long since I've written Antonio a letter, I scarcely know where to begin."

As if to warm up, he started to address the envelope: Reverend Antonio Quevedo, S.J. Then he paused and frowned. *"Dios mio!,* what is his address in Puerto Rico! Daria, will you ask Mrs. Quevedo . . . ," but as he raised his head, he saw that Daria had gone. "Well, I'll get that later," he mumbled; "the letter is the important thing now."

He wrote:

My dear Antonio: It has been a long time since I have written you. I live such a busy life every minute of the day (and sometimes, of the night). I am sure you understand this and will excuse my silence. However, there are moments in life when, busy as we may be, we must take time out to communicate with those we love. This is the case with me today. . . .

Doctor Quevedo tells Father the details of Teresita's vocation and then continues:

You know without my telling you, Antonio, that I shall do nothing to stand in her way. Both María del Carmen and I consider her vocation a blessing from God. At first, naturally, her mother suffered deeply; she was afraid that Teresita, at seventeen, may not realize the step she is taking. Now, however, we both are sure that our child is fulfilling God's will. Our faith moves us to give what God asks, just as Teresita's faith inspires her to respond to His call.

All this, nevertheless, does not completely ease the pain we feel. If it did, the sacrifice would be too small, I suppose. We dread the hour when we shall have to part with this angelic child, Antonio. You will never know what she means to me.

Teresita has, of course, our blessing, and in February we will place her completely in the hands of her Tía Carmen. May God bless my dear child!

I do not want you to write me a letter in reply, Antonio. Instead, I would like Teresita to have one from her Uncle Antonio, waiting at the novitiate the day she enters. With the special grace that you receive in your state of life, you will be able to console her better than anyone at the hour of separation from her family. Moreover, if you help her take the first step toward holiness, I will be more than pleased.

The family sends love and prayers and here goes a strong embrace from your brother,

Calixto.

CHAPTER VII

Off to Be a Saint

IT DID not seem possible that Mrs. Quevedo and Carmen could be packing Teresita's trunk. But there they were, in her bedroom, sitting on the floor alongside the trunk and arranging the religious trousseau.

"We must pack the trunk, Carmen, so that Teresita can remove what she needs without upsetting everything in it." Mrs. Quevedo said this as she folded some cumbersome petticoats. Carmen did not answer; she was busy trying to brush away the tears—they were baptizing her sister's black stockings—without her mother seeing her.

Approaching footsteps brought Teresita into the bedroom. She smiled at her mother, at Carmen and sat near them on the floor. She looked around at everything in the spacious room as if she were taking an inventory of the things that had helped to make No. 7 Plaza de Oriente such a lovable place to live. What she took in was utterly simple. The room and everything in it was of Basque style. There were mahogany twin beds. Over one hung a picture of the Holy Family;

over the other—in which Teresita slept—was a picture of Christ under which was written: "Suffer the little children to come unto me." Her bureau was a large mahogany piece, perfectly plain, whose dominant adornment was a statue of the Child Jesus. A night table, placed between the beds, matched the bureau and held a statue of Our Lady and a small lamp. There were several mahogany chairs in the room and an armchair whose flowered chintz matched the bedspreads and drapes. Tailored curtains covered the windows and the French doors that opened onto a balcony. The largest piece of furniture in Teresita's bedroom was a mahogany wardrobe with full-length mirrors. Teresita had always kept her room tidy, but today the trunk and her new trousseau had cluttered it a bit.

Carmen broke the silence with: "A penny for your thoughts, Tere."

Teresita rose, walked over to her mother, peered into the trunk and said: "Mama, dearest Mama, you are the most orderly person in the world. How God will love to have you in Heaven! You and Papa are saints." She threw her arms around her mother and kissed her hard.

Carmen knew what this could bring on, so she struck a light vein with: "Well, Tere, you seem to be ignoring me. Luis and I don't rate with you any more. Are you getting fickle? Just because Daria says you are 'flying to Heaven' is no guarantee that you won't need us to help you get there."

"What a tease you are, Carmen!" Were there tears in Teresita's eyes as she gave her sister a hug?

Teresita's joy, however, was soon dampened. One truly clenching experience, one last proof of her stability was necessary. On January thirty-first Doctor Quevedo fell gravely ill.

"We believed Papa was going to die," Carmen tells us,

"and he believed it, too. Papa asked for Extreme Unction, which he received with resignation but with hope of recovery. It was a moment of genuine grief for Teresita.... Happily, as so often happens, Papa gained strength after receiving the Last Sacraments...."

Dr. Quevedo responded to the medication ordered by his doctors, and after several blood transfusions, he was well on the road to recovery. As he passed from the critical to the convalescent stage, the family's attention was gradually redirected to Teresita.

"Listen, Tere," a relative suggested, "even though your father is improving, don't you think you should postpone your entrance into the novitiate?"

But the young girl who so dearly loved her father answered: "Indeed Papa is getting well, and in no other way could I better express my gratitude to God for that than by entering as I planned. Even if he weren't improving, there would be no better place to pray for him than in the novitiate."

Her last weeks at home were spent mainly with her father. Not until then did they realize that his illness was not a cross at all, but rather one of God's sweet courtesies to Doctor Quevedo and his "Princess." When, in his life as one of Madrid's busiest doctors, would he have found time for the precious hours with Teresita that his convalescence provided?

The Institute of the Carmelite Sisters of Charity receives its aspirants to the postulate several times during the year. One of the entrance periods extends from the twentieth to the twenty-eighth of February. The Congregation was founded on February 26, 1826, and each year the anniversary is celebrated with great solemnity. The founders of the Community wanted to have as many of the new postulants as possible witness the celebration which so perfectly expresses the spirit of the Institute. Teresita agreed.

"But tell me, Teresita, why do you want to enter precisely on February twenty-third?" questioned Doctor Quevedo.

"Well . . . because, Papa, two and three are five."

"Yes, that's true. But what does five have to do with it?"

Teresita smiled. How could she expect her father to fathom the meaning of her "five." "Look, Papa: M-A-R-I-A," she said, counting 1-2-3-4-5 on her fingers. "Five. In honor of the number of letters that spell Our Lady's name!"

That was not the only example of Teresita's mystical meaning of five. In the novitiate she often used the number five in her devotional exercises: five acts of mortification . . . five Hail Marys . . . five visits to the Blessed Sacrament . . . five acts of kindness! She called it her devotion to the Name of Mary.

Childish, some said. Perhaps, but those small details of love for Our Lady led her to triumph, to a complete renunciation of self. The trifles in life can build up to great virtue.

"When are you entering, Tere?" her brother Luis said.

"The twenty-third, Luis."

"How do you feel, now that the time is drawing near?"

"Very happy! It is going to be the loveliest day I've ever known. And if Our Lady wants to add a favor to the day. . . ." She broke off abruptly.

"What is it, Tere, tell me!"

"I would like my entrance day to be completely white, Luis. I wish Our Lady would send snow on the twenty-third."

February twenty-second dawned—clear—warm—serene. The Castilian sun was beating down on the patio of the Quevedo home, where Teresita sat chatting with her friend Amparin. The latter expressed surprise at the pretty clothes Tere was wearing and said that she would expect a girl to be less meticulously groomed on the vespers of her entrance day.

"A religious vocation does not spell gloom, untidiness or bad taste, Amparin." Teresita's defense was strong. "Don't you think God loves beautiful things? Isn't Our Blessed Lady called the Lily among lilies? I have always liked to dress well, Amparin, but this will end when I enter the convent. I will leave the world on the novitiate doorstep because I want to become a saint. No half measures for me!"

"What a beautiful day it was," commented Luis that evening.

"And the night is beautiful, too," Tere answered; "snow was never more remote."

Our Lady was going to ask much of Teresita from that day forward and, Mother that she is, she wanted to give her child one more proof of her love, one final caress as she left home. Thus, when Tere awoke on the morning of February twenty-third, she looked out on a snow-covered city. Entranced, she stood at her bedroom window thanking Our Lady. It was not until Carmen's voice called: "Hurry, Tere, we can't wait any longer," that she realized she should be dressing for Mass. The family, including Tía Josefina, was in the car when a breathless Tere joined them. They drove to Saint Francis Church, where they had united their voices at the Holy Sacrifice through the years. Doctor Quevedo did not take his eyes from his little Princess, and the tears that she shed did not escape him. Were they tears of fervor and consolation from the intimate embrace of Eucharistic union? Were they tears of emotional appreciation to Our Lady of the Snow? Or were they the tears of parting from father, mother and family? Doctor Quevedo wondered.

It was three P.M. The new postulants were told to report to Our Lady of Mount Carmel Novitiate before four o'clock.

The Motherhouse is on the outskirts of Madrid in a section called Carabanchel, a distance from the Quevedo home. The family assembled, Don Calixto drove his green Studebaker to the Academy to pick up Teresita's aunt, Sister Teresa, and Mother Maria Teresa Rodriguez, the Superior, who wished to be present when Teresita launched her new life. As the car slowly rolled along the streets of Madrid toward Carabanchel, skidding here and there, Sister Teresa complained: "I don't know why we had to have snow today after the beautiful weather of yesterday. I hope Teresita didn't ask for it as Saint Thérèse of Lisieux did once."

What an occasion that would have been for a less perfect soul to make known Our Lady's indulgence toward her! But Teresita only replied: "I like snow very much."

The Mistress of Novices at Carabanchel is, as we have said, an aunt of Teresita and a sister of Doctor Quevedo, a few years his senior. She is a well-balanced person, but perhaps slightly inclined to be more mother than novice-mistress. She knows how to make the mortified life of her charges interesting and happy, while at the same time she forms in them the strict observance of the Holy Rule.

Two people in particular attracted the attention of the Mistress of Novices as the family group filed into the reception room that brisk February afternoon. One was her brother Calixto, still worn from his severe illness. The other was Teresita, serene and very beautiful. She wore a Scotch plaid woolen dress with matching hat and a tailored coat of navy blue. Mother had scarcely made that scrutiny when young voices in the vestibule drew her from the parlor. It was Tere's group from the Academy, come to congratulate the new postulant. As the girls gathered about Tere, each member of her family struggled to maintain a valiant front. Luis looked at his sister wondering, perhaps, what he would do without her infectious laughter at home. Her father, though he tried to keep up conversation, fell into thought from time to time and found himself staring. Carmen and her mother wept. Only Teresita remained composed.

This seems like the propitious moment, thought the Mistress. She interrupted the chatter with: "Now, Teresita, will you come with me?" Turning to her family she said: "When we return, Teresita will be dressed as a postulant."

In less than half an hour they returned to the parlor. Teresita was wearing a black, pleated postulant dress, a black elbow-length cape and a small white linen toque on her head. Her hands were modestly crossed under the cape, as directed, no doubt, by her aunt. Tere's blond hair, pink and white complexion and blue eyes were more radiant than ever against the background of black. No one spoke. Befuddled by their silence, the new postulant said: "Well! You make me feel like one of those plaster mannikins in a department store. . . ." A light ripple of laughter broke the tension and cut short what Teresita was going to say.

This is the note to leave on, thought Doctor Quevedo. Last in the line of farewell, he gave his princess a prolonged hug and said, "*Adiós,* my child. Now you're off to be a saint, eh?" Teresita answered, "Yes, Papa. May I have your blessing?" and she knelt at his feet.

An expression of holy satisfaction shone on Doctor Quevedo's face as he blessed his child, slowly making the sign of the cross over her bowed head.

CHAPTER VIII

The Institute

For many reasons Doctor and Mrs. Quevedo were grateful that Teresita chose to enter the Institute of the Carmelites of Charity. To be sure, they were delighted that she followed her four aunts to the novitiate of Carabanchel. Moreover, there were those pleasant associations with dozens of Carmelite Sisters of Charity during her school years. Most important, however, was what the Institute itself represents. Let us take a look.

It must be clearly understood that the Institute of the Carmelite Sisters of Charity is not an active branch of the cloistered Carmelite reform of Saint Teresa of Avila, as some people think. It was founded in 1826 in the City of Vich, Province of Barcelona, by Mother Joaquina de Vedruna.

The opening chapter of the Institute's History reads:

This Institute, called the Carmelite Sisters ot Charity, is a Congregation of religious women, of the mixed (contemplative and active) life and of simple vows, approved by the Holy See. The primary end is the sanctification of its members through the observance of the Constitutions and of the three vows of Religion, and the practice of prayer and mortification. The secondary end is the spiritual welfare of our fellowmen, the education of young girls of all ages and of every social class, the care of the sick in hospitals (only), the care of orphans in orphanages. The Institute is affiliated with the great Carmelite Order and enjoys all the spiritual privileges of same. Its main objective is Charity.

Mother Joaquina wanted to become a Carmelite from the time she made her First Communion. That undoubtedly had much to do with the name of her Congregation. At fifteen she was going to seek admittance to the Calced Carmelite monastery in Barcelona but her father forbade her. He had her future planned. At sixteen she was married to Don Theodore de Mas, a well-to-do Vichian. Their married life was a holy and happy one, blessed with eight children, but disturbingly punctuated by war.

When Joaquina was thirty-three years old, God revealed to her in a vision the death of her husband. He died a few weeks after that vision, in 1816. Shortly after his burial, she moved to a secluded home in Manso Escorial. There she carefully directed the education of her children and prepared her soul for the life of dedication and prayer that God had in store for her.

An old, inspired Capuchin missionary, Father de Olot, was Mother Joaquina's confessor. Under his direction she increased her prayer and penitential life and solved a major spiritual problem: her vocation. Father explained that she could still become a Religious when family obligations were removed. God, however, did not ask her to wait that long. He effected a meeting between Joaquina and the Archbishop of Vich, who was deeply impressed with her humility and piety. That prelate ordered her to renounce her estate in favor of her eldest son and to dress immediately in the religious habit. He gave her the religious vows in his episcopal chapel on the feast of the Epiphany in 1826.

She was a Foundress before she knew it! Father de Olot, whom Madre Joaquina always called the Congregation's Holy Father, took care of all the necessary formalities of the newly founded community of Sisters in Cardona. He secured papal approbation and state recognition; wrote the Holy Rule; organized the constitutions, and directed holy souls to join Mother Joaquina in her life of poverty, penance and humility. On the other hand, Mother's zeal for the formation of her first daughters was tireless.

In 1828, the foundation still toddling, Father de Olot died. Without his spiritual and moral aid, Mother Joaquina suffered a baptism of fire. Our Lord tried her with every tribulation, even to the extreme of being imprisoned for His sake. Her undaunted courage, however, carried her on. She continued founding Houses of Charity, as they were then called, until a Civil War broke out, interrupting her in 1835.

A year later she resumed God's work, this time absolutely alone. Her chief financial backer, the Archbishop of Vich, had passed away. People who evidently had helped her cause only to gain the prelate's favor, turned their backs on the Institute. She was exposed to the most dire poverty and suffered every hardship imaginable. But her labors were indeed fruitful. The last fifteen years of her life brought a wonderful growth of the Institute of Carmelite Sisters of Charity. By 1854, there were foundations in all parts of Spain. By 1954, Carmelite Convents of Charity dotted the Western World and parts of the Orient.

At the age of seventy-one, Mother Joaquina was stricken with a paralysis that claimed her life. She died in Barcelona in 1854. In September of 1881, Mother Joaquina's remains were removed from Barcelona to the cemetery of the Motherhouse in Vich. Her corpse had undergone no decomposition.

The solemn ceremony of the beatification of Venerable Mother Joaquina de Vedruna took place in Saint Peter's Basilica in Rome, May 19, 1940, feast of the Holy Trinity. Her Cause had been introduced at Rome in 1909. The Holy See sought and found proofs of her sanctity. Chiefly they were: the long religious persecution which Blessed Joaquina had suffered in promoting the Institute; her own personal holiness; heroic virtue; and miracles attributed to her intercession.

The introduction of the Cause of Blessed Joaquina was signed by Pope Benedict XV. The declaration of her heroic virtues was pronounced in 1935 by Pope Pius XI. She was beatified in 1940 and would have been canonized by Pope Pius XII on November 23, 1958, had God's hand not delayed it.

Thus several recent Popes have had a hand in moving Blessed Joaquina's Cause toward its glorious end. On April 12, 1959, the Foundress of the Carmelite Sisters of Charity was canonized at Saint Peter's Basilica in Rome by His Holiness Pope John XXIII.

CHAPTER IX

The Postulant

THE postulant, Sister María Teresa as she was called, knelt at the foot of the statue of Our Lady in the novitiate chapel. She made this act of consecration: "O most pure Virgin Mary, Mother of God and my most loving Mother! Prostrate at your feet I thank you for the immense favors you have obtained for me from your Divine Son, especially for the great grace of a vocation to the Carmelite Sisters of Charity. Here I wish to live until death, working tirelessly for the glory of your Divine Son. Shelter me, O Immaculate Mother, within your blue mantle so that I may never stray from the promises I have made to your Son."

From the chapel she was led to the postulate, where other members of her group waited to greet her. Teresita entered the room smiling. One of the Sisters present at the time has said that "during Sister Maria Teresa's years in the novitiate, she never lost the smile nor the tranquillity that marked her entrance to the postulate."

The postulants welcomed her warmly. Sister María Zaboleta, their Mistress, designated at the long oak table the place that Sister María Teresa would occupy during the six months of probationship. After she was seated, Sister gave her a stamped piece of linen in which were wrapped hoops, needles and enough embroidery cotton to produce a lovely bureau scarf. The new postulant spread her materials on the table and threaded the embroidery needle, for she could see that the recreation period was not to be spent in idleness. The chatter of her companions pleased Teresita. Her interest in their conversation had risen to a height, when a bell calling them to prayer brought the recreation period to a close. Teresita gathered her materials and laid them neatly in the table drawer allotted to her use.

As she left the postulate and followed the Sisters to chapel, she was preoccupied. Not once did Our Lady's name enter into our recreation, she thought. In chapel, Teresita knelt before Our Lord in the Blessed Sacrament and resolved to introduce Our Lady into every conversation she would thereafter hold with her Sisters.

On the afternoon of February twenty-fourth, the winter sun smiled upon a group of postulants who were admiring a new statue of Mary Immaculate that had been erected in the novitiate garden. Teresita Quevedo listened to their appraisal of the artist's talents with a satisfied ear. She was, of course, unaware of the fact that, at the very moment, a well-groomed grandmother and a tall, clean-cut engineering student from Madrid University stood on the novitiate doorstep.

The young man's heart was not serene. His hand trembled as he rang the bell. But he was reassured by the *"Buenas tardes, Señora, Señor!"* of the Sister portress, who nodded entrance as she opened the door.

"Muy buenas, Hermanita," they answered, stepping into

the vestibule. "May we see Teresita Quevedo?" inquired the grandmother, as Sister led them to a small reception room.

"Are you relatives?"

"No; very close friends," the boy replied, giving their names. "We did not see Teresita before she left home, Sister. Could we possibly greet her now and present these flowers?" He tore off the green tissue paper and displayed a beautiful bouquet of roses and delphinium.

"Be seated, please, and I'll tell Mother Carmen you are here," Sister said, bending her head over the bouquet to gather its fragrance.

Fifteen minutes later, Mother Carmen sat opposite the grandmother and the young boy, her attention fixed on the story he was telling. . . . Teresita had been his ideal of womanhood. She would always hold the admiration and respect she had inspired in him when they first met—three years ago.

"In fact," he told Mother, "I fell deeply in love with Teresita but she was unresponsive. She acted as if she were completely ignorant of my deep affection for her, and I believe she was. That made it very difficult for me to broach the subject of love to her. One day last summer, however, I mustered up enough courage to tell her I was in love with her. She listened with her usual composure and then she simply disarmed me with: 'What a thing to say!'

"Recently I discovered her intentions to become a nun and the discovery completely shattered my hopes. I wanted to react gallantly, unselfishly. I wanted to go to her and wish her joy and holiness in her new life, but I did not. Last night I met her brother Luis at our fraternity house and he related the details of Teresita's entrance to this novitiate yesterday. When I reached home last night, I was restless, annoyed with myself and with the world. I knew I had to do something to rectify my bad manners. *But what?* Since I could not trust the state of my emotions to anyone else, I confided in my grandmother, who has always known of my regard for Teresita. Well, Mother Carmen, you know the rest. Here we are."

"Yes. Your story interests me. But unfortunately I cannot follow the dictates of my heart. I cannot permit Teresita to come to the parlor today. Our Holy Rule prohibits visits until one month after the date of entrance. If you wish to come on the March visiting day, it will be on the twenty-fifth, I am sure Teresita will be happy to see you."

Mother Carmen read the answer to that invitation in the young man's face. A meeting would not be necessary. He seemed to know that Teresita would place his flowers at Our Lady's feet, that she would bury his desires in Our Lady's heart, and that she would recommend his future to Our Lady's petitions to her Divine Son.

The boy rose and shook Mother Carmen's hand with warmth. Then he turned and smiled on the dear little lady who had come with him to Carabanchel. "Come on, Grandma," he said taking her arm, "we will be just in time for tea at the Ritz."

To those who knew her well it seemed strange that Teresita, never particularly communicative about her personal life, should keep a diary. She began it during her early postulant days. She wrote her intimate thoughts in a small black notebook, simply, without any literary pretensions; indeed with a sprinkling of grammatical errors. But somehow her writing had charm—the charm and freshness of country flowers. February twenty-fifth she made the first entry:

To Jesus through Mary

25th

I have just spoken to our Mother Mistress and I told her I am very happy. She promises to allow me to perform an act of humility on Saturday so that I may have a little gift to offer Our Lady. Today is the first I have seen these acts performed in the refectory and I must say they fill me with devotion. On March twenty-fifth Mother Mistress is going to give me a little penance chain to wear. What joy it will be, my Jesus, to mortify my flesh for You! Most holy Virgin, help me to be good.

26th

The Community feast! This has been a wonderful day and I begged Our Lady throughout the day to make me a saint. I was talking (we had recreation all day) with Sister X and she said that Jesus wants something very great from me. Tomorrow I am going to our Mistress and I shall ask her to correct me severely whenever she sees anything in me that would displease Our Lord, and even though it may seem insignificant, not to let it pass. You will help me, won't you, dear Mother of God? Each day I love you more! Last night I was ill but I feel better today except that my knees tired terribly at prayer.

27th

Today I confided my desire for correction to my dear aunt and Mistress and also to Sister María. I prayed so much for that lady who is sick with cancer and also for our Sister who is suffering with asthma. The morning meditation was strong but it did not inspire me; mental prayer costs me a good deal. I will be patient because I do my best and because I place all my frailties in your blessed hands, dear Mother Mary. With your help I shall do better.

28th

I made the act of humility today and I have said ten decades of the rosary; tonight, falling asleep, I'll complete the chaplet. These are my tiny gifts to Our Lady today. At the meditation on the humility of Mary I realized how little I am! This was the first day I washed clothes since I came and, as I did so, I could not but think of Our Lady washing the clothes of the Child Jesus, so I united myself with her, heart and soul. I also signed a paper today that has something to do with my Academy Diploma. I do not want to study any more but if Our Lady wants it.... Mother most humble, teach me humility.

29th

This morning each of us had to go to chapel for half an hour colloquy. I spent the time with the Blessed Virgin, begging her over and over to make me what Jesus wishes me to be. The morning meditation was on a religious vocation and on God's promise of salvation if one perseveres. I have come here to be a saint, not just to save my soul! By my prayers I hope also to save the souls of others. Has Our Lord, as Sister María says, given me graces that He has not given to others? If so, O Mother Mary, teach me to correspond to them!

March 2nd

Mother Mistress called me this morning to see how I am coming along. I told her quite well, g.a.D.,* but I added that the devil never stops trying to ensnare me. I also explained that at times I feel Our Lady's presence near, defending me against his onslaughts; she never abandons me. Mother asked me about the particular examination of conscience; I am working on imitating Our Lady in remembering the presence of God. I am so happy Mother called me! I seem to get along very well with her. Life here grows happier every day. I love to think of how peaceful I shall be at the hour of death. O Holy Family, Jesus, Mary and Joseph, I plead for a happy death for my dear ones and for myself.

3rd

They came from home to see me today: Mama, Papa, Carmen, Tía Josefina and my grandparents. They found me looking well and went away very happy. Poor Carmen couldn't stop crying. I wonder why she does not enter; she is so good. God's will be done! At recreation tonight I was talking with Sister Anita (I love her very much) and she said that little souls sanctify themselves by little acts... just by doing for the love of God the

* *Gracias a Diós:* thanks be to God.

things we do each moment of the day. I must give good example in this!

4th

We have begun the Novena of Grace and I am asking St. Francis to help my Luis pass his courses, to make him good and to teach him to love the Blessed Virgin. The Sisters who are going to Peru came to say farewell today. O my Jesus, do You want me to be a missionary? I would love to go to China but right now I guess You want me to pray hard for the mission in Peru.... Most Holy Virgin, teach me to keep my converse with others good and holy! Tonight we had a Holy Hour. I loved it!

5th

Today I read the letters that Mother gave me some days ago. I did not read them before so as to mortify curiosity—a little gift for Our Lady. Like a good child I must show love for my Mother by bringing her gifts.

And so her diary goes on through the month to the twenty-third of March:

23rd

I am here just a month today. Already I realize the many dangerous situations I have bypassed by coming to the house of the Lord and His most holy Mother. I must correspond much more completely with the immense grace of my vocation during this next month. Oh my good Jesus, I would rather die a thousand times than leave You.

Aside from the family, Teresita's first visitor at Carabanchel was her dear friend and former classmate Consola de Paz.

"Are you really happy?" Consola blurted out as she hugged Teresita and tried to brush away the tears that sprang to her black eyes.

"You cannot imagine what my happiness is like," Teresita comforted her. "The convent is the vestibule to Heaven. If only the world knew it, I tell you there would be not enough convents to house the aspirants. You should see, Consola, how much more complete our devotion to Mary is here than it was at school!"

"She was radiant as she spoke," Consola wrote later. "All our friends who visited Teresita noticed the holy expression on her face. It seemed as if the virtues of Our Blessed Lady were reflected there. Speaking confidentially, she told me that she had offered her postulant life for sinners; she prayed God to lead all sinners to the path of virtue."

The girl who enters the novitiate of the Carmelite Sisters of Charity lives in an atmosphere of charity and joy, where the daily routine apparently runs quite smoothly. The various duties of the new life are learned one by one. Slowly she comes to understand her obligations and glimpses, too, the perfection that can eventually be hers if she remains faithful to them. Besides the Mistress of Novices and the Sister appointed to direct the postulants at Carabanchel, there are, from among the veterans in the novitiate, two nuns selected to guide each postulant. They function more or less like guardian angels and so they are called *angels*. The trio forms what the Carmelites of Charity call the *terna*. They sit together at designated recreation periods, they walk together, talk together; the angels fill in strokes when the postulant fails to grasp a complete picture of some phase of her new life.

Sister Anita Prieto was one of Teresita's angels. She was an edifying young nun and Teresita inclined toward her much more than toward the other angel. When she realized this, what did she do? She tells us in her diary: "I went to our Mother Mistress and asked her not to allow me to become attached to anyone, no matter how holy the person. I preferred to suffer loneliness rather than diminish my love of God. No, mv Jesus, do not permit me to love anyone except in You and in Mary. I want to be entirely and wholly Yours."

Teresita, however, had to face a battle. She was by nature affectionate but she fought it to a victory. The little conqueror told Mother Carmen one day when the combat was over: "Mother, I must tell you that I still love Sister Anita very much but with a detachment that makes me extremely happy. I am so glad you made her one of my angels, for I have learned to conquer my affections . . . a lesson I shall always appreciate. I thought you would like to know this, Mother."

She never knew why, nor did Sister Anita, but very shortly after that admission the assignments were changed and Sister Anita was no longer Teresita's angel.

One afternoon the arrival of the Reverend Mother Provincital was announced, and the postulants and novices were called to the large salon on the first floor to greet her. Although she knew the Provincial personally through her three aunts in the Community, when the postulants assembled in the long oak-paneled room Teresita slipped into a corner where she would be inconspicuous. Her desire to be unnoticed was remarked by the older Sisters. One of them later told her aunt, Sister Teresa: "It was edifying to see your niece steal into a corner behind the other postulants. I have noticed that she always manages to attract the least possible attention. Humility should flower in such a soul. . . ."

Those were prophetic words. Humility was taking root in the postulant's soul. She surprised her Mistress Aunt one day during a conference when she said: ". . . it doesn't matter to me any more that other Sisters love Our Lady more than I do. All that matters, Mother, is that I love her completely and that our combined love bring great joy to Mary and glory to God. . . ."

Could this be the Teresita whose childhood ambition was

aired in these words: "I want to love Our Lady *more* than anyone loves her?"

Two of the postulants, former classmates of Teresita's at the Academy, remarked the beautiful development that five months in the postulate had wrought in Teresita. She had been lively at school, they said, and her friends could always count on her for fun and a hearty laugh. Nor was she exact about quitting play in favor of the study bell, for silence was not one of Teresita's natural virtues. That is why it amused and edified them to find her the first to stop talking at the sound of the silence bell.

"How do you do it, María Teresa?" one of them asked one day at recreation, after the latter had been reminded of her violation of silence in the pantry by Teresita's placing her finger to her lips.

"Well," replied Teresita, "Sister María Zaboleta told us during our first spiritual lecture that 'silence is the faithful guard over the spirit' and that Saint James says: 'The religious is vain who does not guard his tongue.' I decided then to guard mine with five keys: M-A-R-I-A."

Silence became one of Teresita's favorite virtues.

The monthly visiting day always brought a large group of Teresita's friends to the convent parlor. It became a familiar scene to see the postulant seated in a semicircle of attentive, wide-eyed girls. They would ask questions such as:

"Tell us, Tere, are you really happy?"

"Am I happy!" she would reply. "If you knew how happy I am, you would all come running to the novitiate tomorrow. I am completely at home here."

"What do you do all day?" another would ask.

Teresita would outline the daily horarium of a Carmelite of Charity postulant.

That was as worldly as their conversation became. Those

of her companions who found its simplicity too difficult to digest did not return to Carabanchel.

There are several entries in Teresita's diary about the parlor visits, and they all run in this vein:

> Those visits in the parlor are difficult. I hope, O dearest Mother, that I did not speak to the girls with a levity today that may have displeased you. Please make me ever mindful of my beloved motto: Mother of mine, may all who look at me, see you.

There can be no question of levity in Teresita's parlor conversation, for the Mistress of Novices has said that "Sister María Teresa was really an apostle during her visits to the parlor, not only to friends of her own age, but also to her elders. With the latter she never lost an opportunity to express the gratitude she owed God for the invaluable gift of a vocation to our holy Institute."

In April, Father Guzman, O.S.A., was calling on a friend in the large parlor at Carabanchel. Teresita was entertaining a group of Academy girls only a few feet away. Father evidently overheard a bit of her conversation because on his departure he met the Novice Mistress in the vestibule and said to her jokingly: "I see you have a postulant who can substitute for you during instruction period, Mother." From that day on, he referred to Teresita as the "Doctorcito." * Actually, she was not learned. She was not a preacher, nor an instructor in the popular sense of the word. She was a complete child, fearless and undaunted in her expression of love for Our Blessed Mother.

Teresita was in the prime of her postulant life, perhaps at a peak of first fervor, the evening she sat at her desk in the postulate and wrote the following letter.

* Little doctor.

To my Heavenly Father.

All that you ask the Father in My Name will be given to you. With these consoling words, Your Divine Son entreats us to ask our needs of You, most Heavenly Father. Thus, I humbly beg Your Merciful Goodness to grant me the grace I need in my spiritual life. I do not deserve Your mercy, for I am miserable and weak; but for that very reason I need Your mercy. I ask this grace through the infinite merits of Your Son, Jesus Christ, in all humility and with complete confidence.

Since you are my Father, You know that I am a little slave of the Most Holy Virgin Mary. You also know that since I received Jesus into my heart for the first time, I have never gone alone to Your Eternal Throne. My Mother has always led me by the hand. She has always begged You for my needs. Today, however, I have her permission to go directly to my Heavenly Father.* She is with me in sweet compassion, but I must plead my cause alone, most Heavenly Father.

Humbly I beg for a greater love of Jesus every day and for the humility I shall need to embrace such love. Give me, my Father, blind confidence in prayer and the grace to pray well; the greatest love possible for my most Holy Mother and the ability to communicate it to others; a deep appreciation of my holy vocation and the grace to accept everything as coming from your Divine Hand. Let me die rather than commit a willful fault or deny Jesus and Mary anything that may show my love for Them. Teach me how to live so as to bring my Mother Mary pure delight.

Deign to make known sufficient miracles of our Holy Foundress, Blessed Joaquina, that she may soon be canonized. Bless our Institute with vocations and with new foundations, especially in China. (Your Divine Majesty knows I would like to go there, but Your holy will be done!)

Eternal Father, I pray deeply and lovingly for Mama and

* What Teresita meant by "having Our Lady's permission" here has never been clarified.

Papa, Carmen and Luis, that their path to salvation may be filled with divine love, grace and mercy. Be good to my relatives—all of them—to my friends and to my enemies. May all be saved!

Charity is the keynote of our Institute. Grant me, then, Heavenly and Beloved Father, the sweet amiability of Mary that I may show perfect charity to all my Sisters and to all who come in contact with me.

Last and most important of all, O merciful and just Judge, I plead for a holy death!

Your humble servant,

María Teresa Quevedo.

CHAPTER X

Stepping Stones

WITH the approach of Holy Week, Teresita could not help but recall how she had observed this sacred season when she was in the world. "Holy Week in the convent is so different," she tells us in her diary. On Spy Wednesday evening she wrote:

Today Mother Carmen advised us to observe the three days preceding Christ's glorious Resurrection in a manner that will please the Heavenly Father. We may choose a way in which we believe that Our Lord will receive the greatest expression of our love.

Dearest Mother Mary, please lead your child in a triduum of prayer and penance. Prevent me from speaking a word that is not absolutely necessary. I shall try to imitate the silence Christ teaches us as He stands before His false accusers. Mother has given me permission to wear the waist chain to mortify my flesh for an hour on Holy Thursday and twice on Good Friday. Help me, dearest Mother, to do my best in order to remain constantly mindful of God's holy presence. I would like to make thirty-three acts of love during the triduum in honor of Christ's years on earth. This, however, dear Lady, will have to go "uncounted," for I abhor measuring my love. How longingly Christ awaits the love that His consecrated virgins show Him during Holy Week! Grant, too, that I may fulfill the hope I have of bringing consolation to your Divine Son, Who has suffered so much for me.

Her diary notes of Holy Thursday, Good Friday and Holy Saturday, too, are revealing.

Holy Thursday

I hope, my Jesus, that you have been pleased with my efforts today. I was fortunate to have had two hours of adoration, one this morning and one this afternoon. How sweet were your gifts to me during those hours of prayer! Thank you, my Jesus, but I beg you with all my heart to treat me "like the family" and keep your gifts for others. My only wish is to make You happy, my Lord, by loving You as much as I have the power to love. I wore the chain for an hour today and its discomfort inspired devotion for Your Passion. I did not speak a word except to You all day, but tonight Mother Carmen asked me a few questions and I had to answer them, but I spoke to You in her, my Lord.

Good Friday

We rose at five this morning in order to make an hour of mental prayer before Mass. I spent the hour on Calvary. At two P.M. we had the Seven Last Words, during which I became quite overcome with grief for Your sufferings and death, dear Lord. When we returned from honoring the Crucifix my heart wept with Mary. How different these days are, my Jesus, here in Your house! Now I realize how poorly I spent Holy Week when I was in the world. My Jesus, I repent of it with all my heart. I promise You that my religious life will be one of continuous love and sacrifice.

Assist me, O Virgin Mary, to hand myself over completely to Jesus, who has suffered upon the cross for love of me.

Mother assigned each of us an hour to spend with you today,

most sorrowful Mother. I repeat here what I asked you during that time—make me exactly as God wishes me to be. Don't count the cost!

Holy Saturday

My desires to receive Holy Communion yesterday were not unfulfilled. They prepared me to receive my Divine Jesus more lovingly this morning. If only we could realize God's Sacramental Presence within us! Dear Mother of God, since I cannot adequately thank Our Lord for this precious Gift, will you thank Him for me and ask Him to place in my soul the grace I need to love and serve Him alone. O Mary, teach me to know the value of a worthy Communion.

On the twenty-ninth of April eight postulants who had completed their sixth month of probationship received the Habit of the Institute. The five who had entered in February advanced to their places as senior postulants. In a letter to her aunt, Sister Irene, Teresita tells something of her impressions of the Investiture ceremony, but more about her desire to become a saint.

My very dear Auntie: Our Mother Mistress has commissioned me to write you today. She asks you to excuse her for not doing so as it is impossible. Tía Carmen has no free time.

I read the letter you wrote and I liked it very much, especially because of the message in it for me. Thank you, Tía Irene, for the prayers you mention. I need them because I want to become a saint and it seems necessary for me to do it in as short a time as possible. The more you pray for me, the faster I shall reach my goal, so please do not stop begging God for His mercy.

Each day finds me happier because I am learning to live the life of love. Our Lord is generous with me. I try to be generous with Him in return, by giving Him whatever He asks. Repeatedly I tell Him that my only desire is to belong completely to Him.

The five of us who entered in February remain in the postulate, awaiting the day when we shall become brides of Christ. If you knew how I envied the eight who received the Holy Habit! They have taken a higher step toward perfection. Some day I pray that step will be mine to take. I know I am not worthy of it but I am going to take advantage of the months that remain to 'spruce up' spiritually. No one could wish to please God more than I, Auntie.

You ask me to tell you my impressions of convent life. Most of all, I am impressed with the love that surrounds us. Then with the order. They say that 'Heaven's first law is order' and I understand why. People in the world couldn't imagine the order in the refectory, for example. (That comes to my mind first because I have a dreadful fear of reading aloud during meals.) Holy Week in the novitiate was deeply impressive, Auntie. Those were my favorite days so far.

Each time Mama comes she seems happier about my choice of life. Papa is a prince. He is getting stronger and I thank Our Lord for it. What an empty world it would be without him! Carmen is the only one who seems a trifle sad. It is a pity that God has not given her a vocation, but He knows what is best for my *Chatina*.

I must end this now, Tía Irene, because Tía Carmen wants to write a few words below. Please continue to pray for your niece, who loves you very much and who always begs God's blessings on you.

Greetings to all the Community.

Love,
Teresita.

The postscript that Mother Carmen added was brief:

This child could not be more perfect. Carmen.

A certain responsibility was now given to Teresita and her associates. They had reached the plateau in the religious life of a Carmelite of Charity where each postulant, besides making careful note of her own violations of the Rule, must examine the externals of her companions' daily life. The faults she finds in them are publicly brought to light at a weekly chapter meeting held for that purpose. For the ordinary postulant the initial accusation is usually a grueling experience. Teresita, on the contrary, did not find it so. To her it was a necessary means to perfection. One of her companions states that clearly when she says: "From the day she entered the postulate, Teresita encouraged us to tell her the defects we saw in her, especially those she was not aware of. . . . She was very humble."

Teresita used to say that the manifestation of faults was "a spiritual alms," which a nun should beg, not shun. After her first chapter of faults she wrote in her diary:

> The defects that the postulants have accused me of today are serious. I am going to make note of them here so that I will have them at hand. My progress must be checked from time to time.
>
> 1. Sister Anita said that I talk too much at recreation about things that concern me. The ego.
>
> 2. Sister Clara—that I am entirely too spontaneous and that I use my eyes when I talk. Worldly.
>
> 3. Sister Julia—that I move too quickly, even when I work. Impatience.
>
> I entrust my progress to you, Mother Mary. Do not let me give bad example by repeating these faults.
>
> After the chapter of faults, Mother Carmen told us not to be discouraged, because Our Lord is pleased with effort. How true! Jesus sees things as they really are. No one understands our weakness as He does. He knows we live for His sake, even though we are remiss at times. He sees that we are not able to do anything without Him; that the only merit we have is His. Therefore, He will make sure that our time and efforts are not lost.
>
> Dearest Mother, lead me on so that all my life may be a consolation to you and an act of reparation to the Most Sacred Heart of Jesus. O Mary, I place all my confidence in you.

Until she was taken from her final illness to Heaven, Teresita jotted down her faults. For instance:

I usually arrive *just on time* for Vespers. (Insufficient preparation for prayer robs God of glory that we are bound as Religious to give Him.)

I like to give out news. (Thus others will see that I am well-informed.)

I laugh too much during our recreation periods. (This can be very annoying and can, consequently, violate charity.)

My walk should be more dignified. (I could never picture Our Lady without grace and dignity. I must imitate her in this.)

After Holy Communion I never pray aloud with the others. (Perhaps I should speak to my confessor about this. Is it my will or God's that I follow in private colloquy?)

In conversation, they say, I move my eyes too much. (That isn't religious; in fact, it is immature and artificial. I MUST correct it! It has been called to my attention many times.)

If the topics of conversation at recreation do not interest me, I act weary. (Charity should be a nun's favorite virtue.)

I walk too fast to chapel for morning prayers. (Why do I have to hurry when Christ is with me every step of the way?)

When they tease Sister X I laugh so heartily; it must offend her. (Perhaps I should apologize to her.)

When I have an unusual story to tell, I become excited and raise my voice. (I must conquer this. Our Lady was never loud.)

They may seem like trivial scruples to twentieth-century sophisticates. Indeed, they may even draw a smile from some Religious. They were for Teresita, however, stepping stones to sanctity. The Ideal she tried to reproduce in her life was that of the Blessed Virgin, to whom she had said many times: "I want to imitate your beauty. . . ." Only perfection could reproduce the total beauty of Our Blessed Mother. For this Teresita strove.

On the feast of Saints Peter and Paul, June twenty-ninth, Mother Carmen sent her five postulants to the chapter room where, on bended knee, each one asked Mother General for the Holy Habit. Their petition was neither denied nor affirmed. "The decision will depend upon the results of your first retreat," Mother told them. "You have reached the eve of a retreat which you should make with all the fervor of your soul. If you can withstand the rigors of these Spiritual Exercises and emerge with a greater love for your vocation, my dear little Sisters, then certainly you will be clothed with the habit of a Carmelite Sister of Charity."

Teresita had not waited until June twenty-ninth to pray for her Clothing Day. A glance at her diary reveals the remote preparation she had made for it. On April thirtieth she wrote:

> Sweet Lady, direct me to fulfill God's will during the next two months. What would I do if Mother General should refuse me the Habit! Do not fail your child who has placed all her confidence in you.

Each day during May, we read in the diary, Teresita made a visit to Our Blessed Lady's altar, apart from others, to offer a gift. The gift was a sacrifice she offered to God through Mary that she might be found worthy to receive the Habit. One day it would be a gift of mortification, such as having sat in an uncomfortable position at recreation, at meals or at class. The following day, it would be offerings of piety; another day, acts of self-denial. They went on through the month, thirty-one such gifts.

The first of June her diary reads:

> Dearest Mother Mary, please apply any merits I may gain this month to the souls in Purgatory. . . . Holy Souls, in return, pray that I may be found worthy to receive the Habit. . . . My Jesus, this is the month of Your Sacred Heart—a time, above all others,

to seek the Divine Mercy that never ceases to flow from It. Have pity on me, O Heart of Christ, and mold me to whatever you would have me be on our Clothing Day!

The first of July brought Father Muzquiz and the Spiritual Exercises of Saint Ignatius. Kneeling in chapel immediately before the retreat, Teresita prayed: "My Jesus, give me the grace to make a good retreat. Grant me sufficient light to see clearly all that You desire of me during these days of love. Most Holy Virgin, do not leave me for a moment or I shall fail."

That evening she wrote in her diary:

Conditions for making a good retreat:

1. Absolute silence . . . Recollection.
2. Abandonment to Mary.
3. Generous giving of self to the Divine Retreat Master.

My dearest Mother, you know the desires I have to fulfill these points. Let Jesus ask of me whatever He wishes. I give Him my all. I am in the world only to love and serve His Heavenly Father. No longer do I desire anything for myself, either health or sickness, honor or dishonor, a long or a short life. Nothing, my dear Mother, but God alone.

Teresita's retreat notes are sketchy but they disclose some of the impressions she took from the retreat. She seems to have been struck by certain facts that Father Muzquiz presented on sin. For example, she wrote:

Father spoke to us about sin tonight. As long as we have life, he said, we have the power to sin seriously. A dreadful but true consideration! . . . Oh my Jesus and my most Holy Mother, deliver us from sin which is the only thing that can lead souls to hell. I must pray more frequently that sinners will change their way of life. As Religious we must prevent them from being condemned to hell. With my prayers I hope to save many, but grant, my Lord, that no one be lost through my neglect.

Fervent, Teresita could not conceive of a Religious falling into the state of lukewarmness. After Father's conference on tepidity, she wrote in her diary:

Even if I should become as dry as a stick, I would go on loving You, my God, and praying until You could no longer resist me.

On the fourth day of the retreat Teresita accused herself of a lack of confidence in prayer. She wrote:

I must go to prayer with more confidence by placing myself in Our Lady's care. I will not lose trust any more because I am incapable of lofty contemplation; rather I shall ask Jesus beforehand to supply all my deficiencies. Thus my prayer will please the Heavenly Father no matter how feeble it may be.

She noted the analogy that Father Muzquiz made between the call of Christ to the religious life and the Heavenly Father's invitation to the Wise Men when the star appeared in the East. "Many saw the star," Father said, "but only three followed it. Only three had the wisdom and courage to follow the star that led to love. . . ."

That night Teresita began to write in her diary:

How many souls more deserving than I. . . . (There is a space and then the concluding words:) Thank you, my beloved Jesus, for the predilection you have shown the least of them.

The final day of the retreat dawned.

Today is the day to make a reform of life (she wrote). My dear Jesus, illumine my soul that I may have no doubt about what You inspire me to do.

At the close of that day she finished her notes:

After consulting Mother Carmen and Father Muzquiz and being convinced in my conscience, I know I am ready to fulfill

Your divine will. Bless, O Lord, my intentions, and give me the grace to carry them out with perfection.

When, on the night before retreat closed, the Community had left the Chapel to retire, the eighteen-year-old postulant knelt at the altar rail and vowed *not to commit a deliberate venial sin as long as she lived.* She made her vow to God in the presence of Mother Carmen and the retreat master, Father Muzquiz, who knew her soul intimately and approved of her promise to God.

CHAPTER XI

Sister María Teresa of Jesus

THE Sister Portress was almost run ragged. The doorbell hadn't stopped ringing all afternoon. "There it goes again," she muttered, and hurried off to answer it.

"Is this the novitiate of the Carmelite Sisters of Charity?"

"Yes, it is."

"These flowers are for tomorrow's Investiture. They were sent by friends of Doctor and Mrs. Quevedo. Card's enclosed, Sister."

"Thank you."

Again the doorbell! This time, as Sister opened the door, her eye caught the name of Madrid's outstanding florist on the delivery truck.

"Good afternoon, Sister. I have an order of flowers for the Clothing Ceremony of Doctor Quevedo's daughter. Do I deliver it here?"

"Well no, it would be better to take it around to the sacristy. First door to the left there, please."

An hour later. . . . "Good day, Sister. Is this where a daughter of Doctor Quevedo is going to take the Habit tomorrow?"

"It is, my good man."

"There is a box of lilies in the truck—too large for you to handle, Sister. Where shall I put them?"

To top it all, the Quevedo family chauffeur drove Carmen to the novitiate door in a car bulging with flowers. Where to put them? The Sister Sacristan knew. "An artist, if there ever was one, she has a place in the chapel for every tiny bud," Reverend Mother used to say. And the chapel was a veritable garden of lilies and roses when the Community assembled for prayer the following morning.

Shortly before the Clothing Ceremony, on September 8, 1948, Mother María Gonzalez Acedo assembled the postulants in the novitiate, where she called the roll of names they would be known by in religion. Breathlessly Teresita awaited the sound of her new name. Finally she heard the clear tones of Mother Superior: "María Teresa Quevedo, you will be called in religion Sister María Teresa of Jesus." Her heart leapt with joy. If she had been given a choice, that is what she would have asked: *of Jesus.* She repeated it over and over in her heart . . . *of Jesus . . . of Jesus.* To be of Jesus was the aspiration of her entire life.

At ten o'clock the five postulants accompanied by the Mother Superior and Mother Carmen began a slow pace down the chapel aisle as the choir of nuns intoned the "Veni Sponsa Christi." Each one took her place at a prie-dieu until a nod from Mother Carmen indicated that she should kneel. The interrogation was about to begin, with Teresita's spiritual director officiating. In the name of Holy Mother Church Father Muzquiz asked:

"Sisters, what is it you desire?"

"In the name of God, we ask for the Holy Habit of Our Lady of Carmel. We wish to dedicate ourselves to the service of Our Most Holy Mother Mary, and to attain sanctification."

"Are you determined to comply courageously with the Constitutions of the Institute?"

"By the grace of God, the protection of the Blessed Virgin Mary, and the prayers of the Sisters, we hope to do so."

"May Almighty God, Who gave you this vocation, lead you along the path of perfection."

Then Father Muzquiz ascended the pulpit and delivered an eloquent sermon on the immense joy that the holocaust of those five virgins would bring to the Heart of Christ. When the sermon ended, the postulants filed from the chapel as the choir sang the psalm "Exaltabo te, Domine."

Mother Anita and Sister Teresa waited in the vestry to dress their niece in her habit. Mother Anita tells us that "Teresita kept her eyes downcast as she entered the vestry and was deeply recollected." They were not sure she knew who were helping to dress her until they had finished. "Then," says Mother Anita, "she raised her eyes, thanked us, kissed each of us affectionately and turned to join the four who were waiting to re-enter the chapel for the completion of the ceremony."

Only Our Lord and Our Blessed Lady knew the sincerity with which Teresita surrendered her soul in the following Act of Consecration: "Most Holy Mother and Queen of Carmel, prostrate at your feet and confiding in your promises, I beg to receive from your loving hands the holy Habit of Carmel. May its Blessed Scapular be my shield against temptation in life and a constant reminder of your predilection toward me, the most unworthy of your children. I choose you as the Mother and Mistress of my religious life, placing in your tender care my body, my soul, my progress in perfection, my temporal and eternal destiny. O Mother, do not let me in any way dishonor this holy Habit that I so unworthily receive. Rather permit it to cover me with your own virtue. Hide me in your Immaculate Heart, where I may be imbued with the grace that will make me useful to the Institute. Grant that from today forward I may be faithful in the observance of our Holy Rule, perfect in charity, and that my spirit reside in heaven where it may taste the delights of Divine Love. Grant that after having given the greatest glory that I can to your Divine Son, I may deserve to be brought to the Carmel of eternal delights where, in your footsteps, I may follow the Spouse of virginal souls intoning the new canticle, praising His unutterable mercies."

It was an arduous day for the newly-received, especially for Sister María Teresa of Jesus. Besides her immediate family, numerous relatives, former teachers, classmates and friends had gathered in the parlor to congratulate her. For each she had a smile, a friendly comment and a holy card—a memento of her Clothing Day. After the visitors had left for home, Sister María del Carmen, a former teacher, asked, "Are you happy, Teresita?"

"To say that I am happy, Sister, is an understatement. I am supremely happy. One could not be happier. I had never imagined that so much bliss could exist in the religious life. My only regret, Sister, is that I did not enter long ago."

Twilight was softly falling on Carabanchel as the five new novices were officially led by Mother Carmen to augment the number in the novitiate. Throughout the welcome ceremony, which consisted of a sisterly embrace from each of the senior novices, the favorite hymn of Sister María Teresa of Jesus was sung over and over:

Quiero, Madre, guardar pura la flor
que ante tu altar un día te ofrecí.
Quiero vivir abrasada en tu amor
para agradarte y parecerme a ti,
O María! *

The Marian flavor of that welcome must have deeply moved Teresita because she referred to it so often when she spoke of her Clothing Day. "And I particularly remember," she would add, "how warmly one of the novices embraced me, whispering in my ear as she did so: 'You must love Our Lady very much!' I like to believe that the Blessed Mother put those words on Sister's lips to assure me of her own welcome as I entered the novitiate."

Alone in her cell after the fatigue of a day filled with emotion, Teresita sat on a little wooden stool caressing her Scapular. She had listened so many times to the reading of the Holy Rule: "The Sisters are commanded to kiss the Holy Scapular with affection and devotion. . . ." As she dwelt on those words, she wondered if the kissing of the Scapular ever became routine! For a moment she was filled with anxiety. Then she promised herself: That will not happen to me, for Our Lady will never fail me.

Before retiring, Sister María Teresa of Jesus wrote in her diary:

Most Holy Mother, Queen of Carmel: I have been so deeply moved by the generous promises you have made to us today, when we received the holy Habit and pressed your sacred Scapular to our hearts, that I have not properly told you of the gratitude and love that fill my heart for you, my dear Mother Mary. From this day forward you will be the absolute Mistress of my

* I wish to keep pure the flower of love which I have placed at your feet, dearest Mother . . . I wish to live burning with desire to please you and to imitate you, O Mary!

life. I have just placed my body, my soul, my progress in perfection, my temporal and eternal welfare into your hands so completely that they are no longer mine. They are yours.

Sweet Mother, you will never let me dishonor the Habit I have received today, even though my unworthiness is sufficient to do so. I am completely confident that you have adorned my soul with your own virtues, as you placed your precious Scapular upon my heart. Grant that this Scapular may be my shield in life, my shroud in death and a constant reminder forever of your favor toward a most unworthy daughter.

Hide me away in your Immaculate Heart. That is the only place where I shall be of any use to the Institute. Only in your heart, dearest Mother, will I have the courage to live a life of faithful observance of the Rule and of perfect charity. Only through your heart will my actions emerge sufficiently purified to bring glory to your Divine Son. Only from your heart will I merit a transfer to the Carmel of Eternal Delights—the Carmel where Jesus awaits the virgin souls who, with a new canticle, will forever praise His unspeakable mercies.

Your,

María Teresa of Jesus

Eight days after the Investiture each new novice received her Holy Rule book from Mother María de Gauna, the Reverend Mother Provincial. It was a simple ceremony in which Mother stressed the significance that the Holy Rule should have in the life of a Carmelite of Charity. Her message was received earnestly by those ardent young souls. Teresita remembered especially the words: "Keep the Rule close to you. . . ." During recreation that afternoon, she took her Holy Rule book from the desk in the novitiate and, holding it close to her heart, said to Sister Margarita, "We must keep this very close to us, as Mother Provincial said. I was thinking, Sister, that if we fail while holding it close, what would happen to us if we should keep it out of sight?"

The Holy Rule book became Teresita's constant companion. During the Christmas holidays her uncle Pedro and his three-year-old son paid Mother Carmen and Teresita a visit. Mother wanted them to see the Crib, so she took little Pedro by the hand and, nodding to his father, led them toward the chapel. She said nothing to Teresita, who, according to the Carmelite of Charity custom, remained behind in the parlor.

They were admiring the Crib when little Pedro said to Mother Carmen: "Auntie, where is cousin Tere?"

Puzzled for a moment, then realizing what had happened, Mother said: "Goodness! I forgot to tell her to come with us. She must be alone in the parlor."

Teresita, however, had not been offended by Mother Carmen's thoughtlessness. Neither did she object to a few moments of solitude. When the guests returned to the parlor, she answered her aunt's "What were you doing here by yourself?" with a casual: "I was reading the Holy Rule, Tía."

During January Teresita caught a severe cold, which settled in her chest. It gave her superiors concern because she ran a fever that kept her in bed longer than it normally should, so Mother Carmen called Doctor Quevedo in to have a look at her. As her father was making a respiratory examination, he rested one of his hands on Teresita's pillow and struck his palm on a hard object.

"What are you doing, child, sleeping on bricks?" he said, quickly pulling up his hand.

Teresita slid her hand under the pillow and pulled out a small black book. Holding it up she replied: "Heavens no, Papa. It is my Holy Rule."

The nurse who had accompanied Doctor Quevedo to the infirmary was a practical nun and had no time for "oddities" in her charges, or in anyone else as a matter of fact. Therefore, Mother Mistress, who also witnessed the incident, expected repercussions as soon as Doctor Quevedo left. She was surprised, however, to see Sister go calmly on carrying out the doctor's orders, then off to the clinic without mentioning Teresita's Holy Rule book. Mother's curiosity tempted her. She gave in and followed Sister to the clinic. Sister was sterilizing a hypodermic needle when Mother Carmen, sounding casual, asked: "What do you think of our little Sister?" The nurse knew perfectly well that Mother was not referring to Teresita's state of health, as she smiled and replied, "The love that your niece expressed in her action was not just play acting, Mother. Ordinarily I would call such a demonstration false piety, but I believe in Teresita. I believe that our Holy Rule is her way to sanctity."

"As it should be for all of us," said Mother Carmen softly, as she walked away mulling over the words of the common-sense infirmarian.

Above all others, Teresita loved Rule 76 on devotion to the Blessed Virgin Mary. Whenever she was sent to read to the aged or sick Sisters, she would open the Holy Rule book first to read the required daily chapter. Invariably, they tell us, Teresita would read Rule 76. At the conclusion, she would kiss the little black book and ask with a smile: "Isn't it beautiful, Sister?"

One day, in order to try her, one of the infirm Sisters forbade her to read Rule 76 again. Sister emphasized the fact that since Teresita had read it to her so many times she had memorized it. Teresita made no comment. Opening the Rule book at random, she read Rule 60 which treats of "Christ, the Model of Obedience."

"You should have seen the expression on her face as she read," the nun remarked to the infirmarian. "Why, that little

Sister gets absolute pleasure from reading our Rule. I usually feel remorseful. I wonder what her secret is?"

"If you ask her," replied the infirmarian, "I'm sure she will tell you that it is the Holy Rule itself."

The novices were given a copy of the Act of Vows to study. Mother Carmen instructed them on the manner of approaching it. . . . "Concentrate on a paragraph of the Act each day," she told them. "A Jesuit priest will be here to open the course on the vows next month and I would like you to be familiar with this matter before that time. It will help you, Sisters, to determine whether or not you can live the life Christ demands of a spouse who professes Poverty, Chastity and Obedience."

One of Teresita's companions grew disturbed when she studied the section of that Act which reads: "With resolution I determine to make an entire sacrifice of my life to God. I promise to observe the Constitutions with absolute punctuality, and to deliver myself over to the works of the Institute with the most fervent charity." She approached Teresita during a recreation period one afternoon and asked if she might speak with her privately. Fearing that it would look odd if they were to go off into a corner of the novitiate, Teresita suggested they ask permission to walk in the garden. Mother readily granted the permission.

"Do not think I am unhappy," the distressed novice said as they walked in the garden; "I am merely worried about the state of perfection in which we are expected to live after we make our vows. Doesn't it disturb you, Sister?"

"I was frightened when I began to study the Act of Vows," replied Teresita. "In fact, I was upset for several days; upset because I, too, dwelt upon the idea of perfection. Then I decided to read on. When I reached the part of the Act that reads: 'Confiding in the protection of Mary, my most Holy Mother,' a profound peace possessed me. I don't know how to explain the peace that came with those words. I am no longer afraid, Sister, for I know that when I do something in the future in a manner less perfect than it ought to be done, Our Lady will supply my imperfections with her perfection. *Hermanita,* when you feel afraid, or distressed, talk it over with Our Blessed Lady. Place your fears in her hands and ask her to adorn your imperfect works with her final touch before presenting them to God. We know that she will never fail us."

Ever after, when those two novices passed each other on the stairs, one would whisper: *"Madre mia,"* and going along her way each would continue in her heart: "take me by the hand and do not ever abandon me."

María Teresa Quevedo joined the Carmelite of Charity Institute with a desire to become a missionary Sister and she had expressed her wish to the Superior General of the Institute shortly after entering the postulate.

On March 12, 1948, she wrote in her diary:

> The Sisters who are going to our mission in Peru have come to say farewell. My Jesus, do you want me to be a missionary? I would like to be one if it is Your holy will. You know, dear Lord, that I would like to go to China, as I have said before, but do with me as You will.

The following week the Institute was informed that the mission they were to take over in China was ready to receive the nuns. This news gave Mother Carmen an idea—she must find out how her novices felt about missionary life. When the novices reported for morning lecture, Mother told them about the mission in China. They responded enthusiastically and Mother grasped the opportunity to tell them that she was going to substitute a class in composition for the lecture period. "Sisters, I would like you to write a paper on 'A Vocation to the Foreign Missions.' Do not hesitate to say what you think. You may make it as personal as you like. Tell me whether you naturally shrink from such a life or are attracted to it. These papers, I assure you, will have no bearing on your future."

Teresita's paper was brief and decisive. "I wish I were indifferent to this question regarding the foreign missions, but I am not. I should like very much to be a missionary and I understand clearly what hardships such a life will offer me," was the core of it. Hoping that her reply might have some bearing on her future life, she signed it with a firm hand. The superiors, she thought, certainly could not mistake her wishes.

That evening Teresita took a cherished holy card from her writing case. It was a picture of Our Lady of the Missions, and the Virgin's features were Chinese. She looked at it lovingly and thoughtfully, then turned it over and wrote: "My dear Mother Mary, if it is your wish, I would like to go to the missions. May God's holy will be done!"

"Regarding the virtue of charity, Teresita was admirable, completely admirable," the Reverend Mother at Carabanchel remarks. "All of us without exception were convinced that Teresita loved us. She seemed utterly pleased when anyone asked a favor of her. Always ready to lend a helping hand, she would mend a toque of the cook Sister, or darn the habit of the laundry Sister, with just as much care and enthusiasm as she would hem the veil of her dear aunt, Mother Carmen.

"Sister María Teresa also loved the sick. There was a novice at that time bedridden in the infirmary. Her illness made her very languid; she didn't care to talk, she didn't like to read, she didn't even want to listen to other people read. She seemed content to lie silently in bed, waiting, apparently, for God's will to be accomplished in her. Although she never expressed it, for she wanted it to come from them, it was Mother Carmen's hope that her novices would volunteer to spend the recreation periods with the sick Sister each day. Mother's hope was not fulfilled as she desired. Only her own niece would daily ask: 'Mother, may I spend one of the recreation periods today with Sister X?' That was a sacrifice because Teresita, above all the novices, loved to chat and laugh at recreation. Yet she would seek the silence of the suffering Sister because she loved charity more than she loved herself.

"No one ever saw Teresita with a long face, either," Mother continued. "If at times she appeared serious due to religious custody,* one would only have to ask a favor of her to see a smile light up her countenance.

"Teresita was prudent, extremely prudent for her age. She naturally loved Mother Carmen but always held herself aloof from her in the novitiate. She told me once that as far as she was concerned, none of the novices need know she was Mother's niece. She did not deny, however, that this sacrifice cost her more than she cared to admit, because it was not easy to hide the deep affection she had for Mother Carmen."

Saturdays and vigils of Our Lady's feasts were days especially dedicated to works of charity in Teresita's spiritual world. "Little gifts for Our Blessed Mother," she used to say. If ever there was a time when Teresita's natural impulsiveness was evident, it was on Saturday. She would go, un-

* Custody is a mortification of the eyes. It is keeping the eyes cast down to curb curiosity.

seen, from locker to locker shining the Sisters' shoes. Then to the laundry to capture torn stockings and darn a few pairs before the weekly wash would be returned to the nuns. A dozen other kind acts of charity would pass through her eager hands before the day was done.

It was commonly known among the novices that whenever Teresita was chatting in a group, the conversation was on the highest plane of charity. If it weren't, she promptly did something about it. On one occasion, she heard a novice say that Sister so-and-so never contributed generously to the general recreation periods, but that she could be seen laughing and chatting with everyone's family and friends on visiting days. Teresita grew pale at that small remark. "It can't be, Sister. I don't believe it," she protested. "Sister is very dignified in the parlor. I've seen her there with her family and she behaves modestly. In fact, last week Mama remarked her poise."

"Thank you, Sister." It was Sister so-and-so, who during the conversation had entered so quietly that no one noticed her. "You are so kind, Sister María Teresa." Then, bursting into tears, she turned and walked over to the window, away from the group. Teresita followed and tried to comfort her. "Sister, don't cry. You will make Our Blessed Lady very happy if you offer this hurt to her. Perhaps you have nothing else to give her at the moment but this misery. Give it to her then, *Hermanita.* If you can't give it all at once, give a little today, more tomorrow, until it is all placed in her understanding heart."

It warmed Teresita's heart to see the Sister's face serene again. Teresita was always grateful to Our Lady when she allowed her to help others find peace. That was her recompense. She also enjoyed any expression of surprise that followed her acts of charity. In the case of shining the nuns' shoes, for instance, she loved to hear them ask at recreation: "Who shined our shoes?" or "Who mended our stockings?" Amused, she would bend painstakingly over her embroidery, pretending to know nothing about it.

Such was the tact of Teresita in the service of her Sisters.

CHAPTER XII

Her Little Sack

TERESITA worked earnestly toward becoming a saint. One would think she had some kind of premonition of the short life Almighty God had marked for her. Just a month and a half after taking the Habit she wrote in her diary:

I have seen clearly what I must do to become a saint. I had been apprehensive about the way I was using time, for I realize that no fraction of the important years in the novitiate should be lost. However, after consulting an authority (Father Muzquiz) on the spiritual life I feel completely at ease about my distribution of time. Father makes the ascent to sanctity seem quite simple. He explained what I must do to be a saint and I intend to take advantage of every point he listed, after, of course, recommending myself to Our Blessed Lady. She will lead me to whatever Jesus wills every moment of the day. Nevertheless, I must examine my conscience on the following points every evening:

1. No matter how slight they may be, imperfections must be avoided.

2. When filled with defects, one should not become discouraged. Rome wasn't built in a day!

3. If one falls, she must place herself under Our Lady's cloak immediately.

I have been thinking lately that it would be a good idea to have a spiritual sack into which the day's works may be placed. Every evening I could bring it to Our Lady and ask her to remove the defects. Free from flaws, I would take the sack to His Eucharistic Presence and offer it to Jesus. I shall do this! Years from now, when the sack is full, I believe I will have reached sanctity. O my Mother, I know you will help me. I also know that it will take the rest of my life to fill the sack.

The "sack" became a valuable spiritual tool with Teresita and as time went on she introduced it to her Sister friends. Teresita tells us that Sister Guadalupe Fuentes, downcast because she felt that her struggles toward perfection were unrewarded, confided in her, hoping for a bit of good advice. This is the counsel Teresita gave her: "Sister Guadalupe, I am glad you have told me about this; I see that you want to be a saint just as I do. Father Muzquiz says we must never become depressed by our failings. I notice that discouragement is the root of your present dismay, isn't it? You say you are filled with imperfections. Well, maybe you are! Aren't we all? Why don't you try this; some of the Sisters have found it helpful. Create two spiritual sacks and put your imperfections in one of them. Take one imperfection at a time from the sack and work on it until you overcome it. Ask Our Lady to help you. When you have conquered the fault, place the opposite virtue in the empty sack. It is amazing, *Hermanita,* how quickly that empty sack will fill out. Don't be discouraged any longer. You have a remedy now and remember that the Blessed Virgin, who never fails us, is always on hand to help."

One day when Teresita was taking an inventory of her own sack, she felt gratified about the way it was beginning to fill out. Perhaps the gratification was a fleeting shadow of vainglory, perhaps it was not, but it disturbed her. She confided her disturbance to Father Muzquiz and he asked her why she attached so much importance to it. "Because, Padre," she answered, "vainglory seems to be at the core of so many good desires, like the little worm that is at the core of a beautiful apple. And you know how that worm can spoil the apple! Those are Satan's subtle ways of making inroads. We can never be careful enough, Padre."

"Your niece is a real child of God," Father told Mother Carmen as he was leaving the novitiate that afternoon. "How these simple souls put us to shame, Madre!"

The Carmelites of Charity have many lovely customs, but one in particular is appealing. They salute Our Lady at the striking of the hour with: "Blessed be your Purity, O Mary!" after which they pause for a moment to make an act of spiritual communion. If devoutly followed, it brings the soul directly to the presence of God many times a day. Teresita told Mother Carmen that she "loved to bless the hour" because that practice had been "her best teacher of recollection" and she was trying to fill her sack "with recollection these days." That was November of 1948.

How did she make out? We'll let someone who watched her at close range tell us. The Mistress of Postulants says: "I used to be edified to see Sister María Teresa so recollected. It cost her a great deal to master the virtue of custody of the eyes. She told me, however, that once she learned to fix her glance on the sweet face of Jesus, it was difficult to raise her eyes, even to pass something at table in the refectory."

Do we need more evidence? If so, here it is.

A Sister junior to Teresita said: "I remember noticing Sister María Teresa of Jesus the first evening I went to the refectory. I could not take my eyes off her during the reading because she seemed to be completely in another world. She never lifted her eyes, not even when she passed the food. I was fascinated with her composure and before retiring that night I prayed for the grace to imitate her."

From Sister María Teresa's diary we learn that her edification in the refectory that evening was not casual:

The new postulants arrived today. They are going to observe me just as intensely as I used to observe the novices when I entered. Do not permit me, Sweet Lady, to disedify them. May all my actions be only for the love of Jesus and you, my dearest Mother! I shall pray to you in the refectory.

Was Sister Maria Teresa's life completely without suffering? Up to this moment it may seem that she was a favored child, nurtured from the cradle in an atmosphere of affection and love, carried through the postulate on wings of grace, and raised to heights of sanctity with wonderful ease. But that is not the way of holy souls, nor was it the way of Teresita.

Untold periods of spiritual aridity racked her soul. Indeed, her little sack could never have been completely filled if it hadn't had a good portion of the virtue that grows out of suffering! In the Spring of 1949 she wrote in her diary:

First Day.

Today I told Mother Carmen I must see her when she can find time to see me. I cannot pray of late and I find our spiritual duties a difficult task. I was actually happy today that we did not have to continue the long devotions. . . . I am ashamed to admit that, but it is a fact, and I must make it known to Mother.

Second Day.

Mother asked me in passing today if the matter I asked to see her about yesterday is urgent. I told her it can wait, because I know she is very busy. She will send for me tomorrow. . . . I hope so! . . .

Fourth Day.

Retreat opened today. The first meditation I made was fair . . . the second was poor, very poor. I could not meditate. . . . I could not recollect myself at all. O most Holy Virgin, you know I do not want to waste time; please help me. My poor little sack is empty!

Teresita was submerged in a sea of confusion. As the retreat progressed, she seemed to become more and more disturbed.

Fifth Day.

The examination of conscience today brought to light my failures in the virtue of silence. It seems I was much more perfect in this regard a year ago. But what can I expect! When recollection goes, silence goes with it. My soul is weary and restless. O Mother Mary, I beg you to help me. Do not leave me now when I need you most. You know I love you and want to please Jesus through you. Help me, then, to do better regardless of what I may have to suffer to conquer myself. Bless me, dearest Mother.

Sixth Day.

My efforts to do good are useless, dear Mother Mary. Pardon my imperfections! This failure to please you and Jesus deeply humiliates me. I am so weak that it has become difficult to see the good intentions in anyone. Give me eyes of charity that I may see things in a pure light. It really grieves me to be so badly behaved, Most Holy Mary.

Seventh Day.

What can be the matter with me! I am an utter failure spiritually and I don't know why, dear Mother Mary. Give me the light to see clearly and the grace to correspond to all that Jesus desires of me. O Mary, how flat my little sack has become!

Eighth Day.

Sweet Lady, I have been strongly tempted. There are moments when I do not even want to be good because Satan makes me feel that my wish to become a saint is vanity. Sweet Mother Mary, I beg you, do not let me be lost! I confide completely in you.

Was Teresita failing spiritually as she says? There is no doubt that she was failing physically. May of 1949 stole the little Sister's perfect health and left a weakened body that would never again regain its former strength. Perhaps her physical maladies played havoc with her spirit, but it is much more logical to maintain that God was trying Teresita's spirit in the fire of love. He wanted her to feel the weight of self-vanquishment and thereby teach an eloquent lesson of holiness. She knew the struggle of temptation. She suffered untold agonies because of the weight of her sins. But if it were not for her diary, most of this would never have been discovered. In the eyes of the Community, "she was always the same charming, virtuous little nun that they received on her Clothing Day."

In a letter written September 16, 1949, Teresita gives her dearest friend, Sister Antonia Orozco, only a hint of her interior struggles. Her tone is chatty and joyous throughout:

My dearest Sister in Jesus and Mary, It has been a long time since I have written you, so you can imagine how deeply I am going to enjoy the time allotted me to write you this afternoon! Since my Clothing Day you have heard nothing about my life here. If only I could see you personally, *Hermanita,* I would tell you a million things; I am so dull on paper, as you know.

My life here has been filled with beautiful examples of holiness and virtue. Only a very foolish Sister would not try to imitate the fervor and the enthusiasm for perfection that surrounds us on all sides. I am earnest about being good and everyone here tries to help me. But since I have had little experience I do not always make the grade. That does not mean that I lose hope of becoming a saint, *Hermana.* I have come here for that reason, and I am sure Our Lady will help me to accomplish my purpose because it is God's holy will.

I have not had any great difficulties. Our Lady has been trying me since the month of May and I am accepting her little trials with love and gratitude. I will not deny that I have a few dark moments, but all those things pass away and God's goodness alone remains.

My desires to make a holocaust of my life to God are tremendous. *Hermana,* pray that I may accomplish this.

You are in my prayers every day. . . .

Greetings to the Community,

Your loving

María Teresa of Jesus.

P.S. The next time I write, I will tell you about my little spiritual sack.

CHAPTER XIII

Code of Amiability

THE first year as a novice was over. Teresita and her sister novices had advanced to the senior novitiate. This is a year in which the novices prepare for their future life of teaching, and they spend four hours a day in class. It must have cost Sister María Teresa a great deal to meet the textbooks again. She does not remark it, however, in the only comment that we have of her second year of noviceship.

I have entered the senior novitiate, led by the hand of the Blessed Virgin Mary. She will help me increase my observance of silence, recollection, poverty, and exact obedience. I am sure that if I unite my soul with Christ's every hour of the day, I shall meet no grave obstacle in the attainment of my goal. Our embroidery will be set aside this year because we have to dedicate ourselves to study. Sweet Lady, my life is in your hands.

Teresita wrote that in her diary in 1949.

Teresita's companions tell us that she "gave herself to her studies that year with the same fervor she put into everything that represented the will of God." And that "she had such complete control of her inclinations, one would think she highly favored study."

Sister María Luisa Gonzalez declares that Teresita prepared her assignments with a unique enthusiasm during her second novitiate year. "Her former aversion to study was so powerfully mastered!" Sister said. "It convinced me that her only desire was to do the will of God. Often she used to tell me that Our Lady was her 'treasury of grace.' When she found herself spiritually poor and unable to purchase little gifts for God, she would draw the necessary means from that 'treasury,' which never ran out of revenue. Her love for Our Lady was boundless."

One morning, shortly after that year had begun, Mother Carmen sent a group of senior novices to the kitchen to pare vegetables. Such chores must be performed either in silence or in spiritual conversation. They had scarcely seated themselves, when the less recollected members began a friendly chat. Since they persisted in it, Teresita, shorn of human respect, and with the simplicity of a child, said: "Goodness, I forgot to bring a stool for Our Lady!" She rose and walked out to fetch one. The novices giggled as they watched her pick up a stool and place it beside her own. Rather suddenly the smiles faded. How could they violate the Holy Rule with the Blessed Mother seated in their midst! As if she hadn't noticed their behavior, Sister María Teresa remarked: "Because we are in the kitchen doesn't mean we must separate ourselves from Our Lady, does it? We can please her while peeling potatoes and carrots just as we please her by making a meditation or saying a Rosary." Teresita was so amiable, no one ever thought her officious.

"Do you know how we spent the time?" says one of her

sister novices. "By reciting over and over Rule 76: 'The Sisters of this Institute will have a special devotion to the Most Blessed Virgin Mary, etc.' Many of us are grateful today for that incident in the kitchen for, had we not been graced with Teresita's presence, we may never have committed to memory one of the most beautiful chapters of our Holy Rule. Teresita did all things with the amiability of Our Lady!"

Amiability was Teresita's most characteristic virtue. She drew up a norm for acquiring amiability which she printed on a large card. Painted on the foreground is a picture of Our Lady with the Child Jesus in her arms. Under the image, in Teresita's writing, are the words: "Code of Amiability." It reads as follows:

The virtue of amiability results from the fusion of several strong virtues. It is the 'all things to all men' that grows out of charity; the knowledge of self that humility teaches; the pure detachment found in mortification; the meekness born of patience; and the undaunted courage won of perseverance.

Of what does amiability consist? To be amiable, as the Mother of God is amiable, one must radiate a strong sweetness—one that will bring a smile to the lips of another and invite confidence. Amiability moves one to give in meekly to the wish of another, or to lighten another's burden with a kind and comforting word. It is the priceless fruit of union with Our Lady.

What are the ten commandments of the Code? The Code of Amiability obliges one:

1. To smile until a kindly smile forms readily on one's lips.
2. To repress a sign of impatience at the very start.
3. To add a word of benevolence when giving orders.
4. To reply positively when asked to do a favor.
5. To lend a helping hand to the unfortunate.
6. To please those toward whom one feels repugnance.
7. To study and satisfy the tastes of those with whom one lives.

8. To respect everyone.
9. To avoid complaining.
10. To correct, if one must, with kindness.

These are the dispositions which union with the amiable Virgin will place in our heart.

Such pure love for the Mother of God was bound to be contagious! Teresita's companions have written page after page on their impressions of her devotion to Mary. All of them are as strong and sincere as this of Sister María Belen: "There is no doubt about it, Sister María Teresa communicated her love of Our Lady to us. On recreation days I used to seek her out, if only for a few minutes of conversation, for I knew that I would leave her with increased fervor. What heavenly conversations she held with me! She frequently spoke of Our Lady's amiability with a simplicity that made my heart burn with love. We can truly apply the words 'from the abundance of the heart the mouth speaketh' to Sister María Teresa of Jesus. She was amiability personified. Whenever I left her I felt as if I had made a meditation."

The influence of her love for Our Lady reached beyond the novitiate. This is what her uncle, Father Jesús Quevedo, S.J., has to say about it: "Teresita was a refined soul; amiable and humble. Her desires to please the Blessed Virgin Mary, with whom she enjoyed an intimate relationship, were edifying. In my opinion, her love for Our Lady surpassed the ordinary love of a devotee of Mary. Something about it was contagious. At least it was for me! I have never before had contact with a soul whose devotion to the Blessed Mother influenced my own as did that of Teresita."

On Sexagesima Sunday in 1949, Teresita wrote Father Jesús Quevedo a letter in which we find traces of the amiability after which she patterned her life. It reads:

My dearest Uncle: Since Lent is close at hand, I am sure you will disown me if I don't get a letter off to you before the Holy Season sets in.

I enjoyed the letter you wrote me on the occasion of my Clothing; thank you, Tío. When you mentioned that the novitiate life should cost me very little, you uttered prophetic words. It is true! God asks so little of us. One has to be very alert to avail herself of every opportunity to practice mortification. Six months have passed since our reception day and I often ask myself if I have made good use of them. I want to be a saint more than ever, Tío. They say that sanctity is a question of will. If that is the case I assure you that my will in that regard is strong. Why is it, though, that I have such strong desires to become holy and yet advance so slowly? (If I advance at all!) Perhaps I am too lacking in humility, which is the foundation of sanctity. Humility is difficult to attain, Tío; but I believe I shall obtain it, for I pray for it many times a day and also for occasions to practice it. I always direct my prayers to Jesus through the Immaculate Heart of Mary.

Tío, I am deeply confident that I shall reach the goal of my religious life because of the love I have for the Mother of God. It is consoling to know that my Mother wants to help me become a saint. I feel her presence ever near me.

Perhaps I had better close this letter, for I could go on forever talking about Our Lady and, as usual, Tía Carmen wants me to leave room for her note to you.

Please write me again, for your letters inspire me.

You are always in my prayers, Tío. Will you pray for this poor niece of yours who needs God's grace so much?

Respectful greetings to your Superior and for you an affectionate embrace from your

María Teresa of Jesus.

A year before Teresita wrote the above to her uncle, she had shown a spark of her amiability in a letter to her brother.

Luis was evidently proud of it for, as he walked into the lounge of Madrid University's School of Engineering one March morning in 1948, he beamed as he read her letter. Passing through the lounge, he bumped into one of his fraternity friends. Noticing Luis' wide grin, his friend kidded him with: "Man!, she must be a doll to light you up like that!"

Luis wagered: "Bet any amount of money you don't have a sweetheart as lovable as mine!" Then he confessed, "This is a letter from Teresita. Listen, José!" Luis read:

Dearest Luis: We have begun the novena of grace to Saint Francis Xavier and I am praying for one intention—that you will pass your engineering courses with flying colors. In my daily prayers to Our Lady, I ask her to keep you good. It is important for God to have fine Christian men to carry His torch in the world today. Besides those prayers, I beg the Holy Ghost every day to direct your choice of a wife. Not that I expect you to marry soon! But, who knows? When you do, I want your wife to be someone very special, Luis, because you are very special to me.

Mama, Papa, Carmen, Tía Josefina and our grandparents came to see me on Sunday. They seem very happy—except Carmen. She cried all afternoon. It grieved me to see her cry because she is good and deserves to be happy—so much more than I. Please be more affectionate with her, Luis. You must help her overcome the loneliness that she feels since I have left home. It is dreadful! I know, because I miss her too. It will relieve me to know that you are showing her many loving attentions.

Tía Carmen and I understand each other quite well. I am careful, though, not to make her feel that I expect her to give me more attention than she gives the other postulants. She is like Papa—kind, understanding and holy.

I have been here a month. I realize now that Our Lady wants me to correspond to a very special grace which her Divine Son is about to give me. Will you say a Hail Mary daily for this intention, Luisito? If I grow more holy, you will too, because you are in my heart.

I hope you will be with the family next visiting day. I missed you terribly on Sunday. God bless my Luisito!

Love and a hug from

Teresita

When Sister Irene—the youngest of the four sisters of Doctor Quevedo who became Carmelites of Charity—began to read Teresita's Ten Commandments of Amiability for the first time, she paused at the second, smiled, and related an incident that occurred when Teresita was a schoolgirl. The incident shows that her niece had made use of every opportunity that came her way in order to acquire the virtue of patience. Certainly, Teresita knew what she was doing when she gave patience a prominent place in her Code, her aunt thought.

"Teresita was in Vich on October 27, 1947, with a group of girls from our Academy in Madrid," Sister Irene states. "They were on a pilgrimage to the Motherhouse to venerate the remains of Mother Joaquina, our Holy Foundress. I was also there, for I had been sent with the pupils from Caceres, who were also on a pilgrimage. Our girls really invaded the cloister, where the relics and sacred roots of the Institute speak deeply to their hearts. I remember remarking to my companion that Teresita's visit at the altar where Mother Joaquina's remains lie was rather long. 'She must be fascinated with the inscription at the base of the altar,' Sister told me. 'She seems to be copying it in a little book.' I could see then that Sister was correct, so we went on our way.

"In the late afternoon we were preparing for the return trip to our various provinces. I went over to where the Madrid group had been told to meet so that I could say goodbye to my niece. The Sister in charge was checking the roll and echoed my 'Where is Teresita?' with surprise. 'Why I thought she was with you, Sister,' she replied. The search began and lasted two hours.

"Finally, Teresita came along smiling, but behind the smile there was a trace of pain. She had been the object of an annoying search, the cause of an unwelcome delay, and it had distressed her. I rushed toward her and asked, 'Tere, why did you do this?'

"She looked calmly at me. There was a faint smile still on her lips as she replied: 'Tía, I did not do it deliberately. I'm sure I had to practice greater patience than anyone concerned. After lunch, the snap on the collar of my dress dropped off and I asked one of the Sisters at the convent for a needle and thread in order to replace it. Sister brought me to a small parlor and told me to take off my dress and sew the snap correctly. Then she went out and closed the door. I sewed on the snap, put on my dress, and attempted to leave the room but I couldn't get out. The nun had locked the door because there were many visitors about, and she forgot to come back to open it. I've been in that room until this minute, Tía.'

"I admired the composure with which she retold the story to the Sisters from Madrid. It was indeed remarkable—the impetuous child of yesterday was a model of patience today. She not only excused, but amiably excused the forgetful keeper of the keys. And to numberless queries she patiently replied: 'No, I did not panic,' or 'I kept Our Lady's patience in mind,' or 'My only concern during those hours was the trouble I might be causing others.'

"As our bus rolled toward Caceres, one of the older girls in our group said: 'I don't know how the rest of you feel about it, but that Quevedo girl's example was the best part of this pilgrimage for me. I've often listened to sermons on the value of good example, but today I learned the value of it.' (She did not know that Teresita was my niece.) I, also, had to admit to that lesson and to another as well—a young girl's patience in a truly distresssing ordeal."

CHAPTER XIV

Illness and Convalescence

THE Sisters were gathered at recreation in the novitiate. It was April 30, 1949, the eve of Our Lady's month. One novice tried to outdo another in suggesting pious practices or generous acts of mortification that could be offered to the Blessed Virgin during the month of May. Sister María Teresa of Jesus sat quietly admiring the enthusiastic suggestions that each of her companions was making, when she was brought out of her fascination by: "Teresita, you haven't said a word! What are you going to do for Our Lady?"

"I haven't the slightest idea," Teresita confessed. "Usually I know what Our Lady expects of me, but today my mind is blank. However, I'll concentrate more fully on it, for I am sure Our Blessed Mother will ask for a May gift."

The following day she wrote in her diary:

Dearest Mother, your month has begun today. I am ready to do anything for you, but for some unknown reason I am filled with fear. I am utterly without fervor! Help me, dear Mother.

Enlighten me, Holy Spirit, to understand what God wants of me and give me strength to do it.

What has happened to Teresita? Could she in the fullness of her novitiate life be utterly without fervor? Or was it that her body, which up to this time had followed her soul with swift agility, had begun to feel the overwhelming weight of an infirmity? Perhaps Our Lady chose to test the love of her child.

That first of May proved to be a memorable date in Teresita's life. She had prayed to the Spirit of Light: "Make me see what God wants of me." After prayers that evening her eyes were opened. Since she had coughed considerably in chapel during the night prayer, the Novice Mistress was waiting for her in the corridor as she left chapel. "Have you a cold, Teresita?" she asked.

"Oh, no, Madre." And she quickly added, "I am tired. Today I didn't have the ambition to chant office."

"Don't you feel ill at all?"

"No, Madre. Not at all."

"Well, let us see what the thermometer will show," Mother wisely suggested as she led the way to the infirmary.

The temperature Mother read explained the glassy eyes and flushed face of Teresita. Nothing very serious, she thought, and then aloud: "You will have to stay in bed for a few days. Perhaps Our Lady. . . ."

". . . is answering my prayers, Madre," she interrupted her aunt.

"Now I see clearly," she said, as she stretched her feverish body under the cool sheets of the comfortable infirmary bed, "and I bow in humble and loving submission to the will of your adorable Son, dear Mother Mary. Let the month of May be lived by me as He sees fit. I love you, my Mother, very, very much."

During her illness, Teresita's friend, Sister María Josefa, visited her in the infirmary. The latter was thinking of that recreation period during which Teresita seemed so languid and uncommunicative, when she asked: *"Bueno, Hermanita,* have you discovered what Our Lady wants of you during this month of May?"

"She wants what you see, *Hermanita,* a bedridden novice. A novice who must be patient, for she does not know how long this illness will last. But I am not going to question God's holy will, since I want it to be fulfilled in me. Moreover, I am in the hands of Our Lady. No one knows better than she what is best for me. Do you remember how I was wondering what to give Our Lady for the month of May? Well, I am overjoyed that she selected her own gift."

Sister María Josefa left her dear friend that afternoon, edified by her words and by her example. She claims she had meditation material for the next two days. "Teresita knew," Sister adds, "how to accept illness. She did it with the natural grace characteristic of her in health. Her key was fidelity to God's will.... The result of such fidelity was an extreme optimism toward her illness and an amiability toward the visitors to the infirmary."

On the second Saturday of May a young lady named María Dominguez entered the novitiate of the Carmelite Sisters of Charity. María had met Teresita when the Quevedo family used to vacation in Santander, and they became friends while she studied in the North of Spain during the Civil War.

"When I reached Carabanchel," María said, "I was filled with joy, naturally. But when I learned of Teresita's illness I became terribly alarmed. Mother Carmen, however, did a very human thing that day. As soon I was attired in my postulant dress she brought me to the infirmary. There was Sister María Teresa of Jesus! It was almost impossible to believe that she was dangerously ill with a high fever. She sat up in bed, opened her arms wide, and gave me a warm and smiling welcome.

"Our Lady has brought you here, Cusa," Teresita said, using the familiar pet name she had been known by in school, "on the second Saturday of May. That is an important detail. It means that you must put yourself under Mary's protection and grow in God's love under her special direction. You will love Carabanchel; we are all very happy here. I am sorry to have to receive you like this, but I have been a bit lazy of late and the bed is a pleasant refuge. It is, however, God's will, Cusa, to keep me in fetters, so I am trying to fulfill it with love."

It was customary at Carabanchel to prepare the meals for the sick nuns in the diet kitchen near the infirmary. The nurse who took care of Sister María Teresa was a person of frail memory. Invariably she brought Teresita her tray without salt, a cup, a fork, or some other detail necessary to one's enjoyment at meals. Teresita was naturally tried by those inconveniences, but she welcomed them. The infirmarian tells us that when she noticed her negligence, she would offer to return to the kitchen in order to supply the need. Teresita never allowed that. "No, Sister, no, please!" she begged. "Let me practice mortification. I love these little opportunities to do so. I'll make out fine; watch me!" The nurse always gave in, mortified by her oversight. She had to practice virtue herself to cope with Teresita.

"Sister, please bring me a small portion of soup at dinner," Teresita always asked the nurse. It was usually rice soup, and a little went a long way. Perhaps because the nurse felt that rice soup would be nourishing; perhaps because her interpretation of the word "little" differed from that of her patient; undoubtedly because God proposed to try Teresita in those details, the infirmarian never failed to fill the bowl. "An offering of love to Our Lady," Teresita would say, when the nurse would attempt to apologize for the brimful bowl.

One first-class feast day Mother Carmen sent a novice to recreate with Sister María Teresa during the dinner hour. The tray was brought in with the usual large bowl of soup. Teresita looked quizzically about her, for she was not accustomed to visitors during meals, except the infirmarian. The latter nodded. Her patient's little act of mortification had always been performed in silence; today must be no exception. How would Teresita handle this, Sister Jacinta wondered. "With characteristic simplicity," she relates, "Teresita asked the novice to observe a few moments of silence with her while she took her soup; during it they would unite their hearts with the loving heart of Mary Immaculate."

Sister María Teresa noticed how glum the novice was after the silence was broken. Teresita feared that her imposition may have been the cause of it. Rather apprehensively she asked, "What is the matter with you, *Hermanita?*"

The novice looked at Teresita half-surprised, half-relieved. "I am terribly distracted, because I am so disturbed lately, *Hermana.* To come to the point quickly, Sister, Holy Communion has become a grave concern to me. I am not recollected. I am completely cold. I am unresponsive to grace. I feel that I should not receive Our Lord with such dispositions. What would you advise me to do?"

Sister María Teresa was wholly relieved. She replied immediately: "*Hermanita,* if our Communions were completely fervent, we would be saints. That is not God's plan. He wants us to offer Him our hearts and all our works without forcing ourselves to be recollected. Make your offering in humble simplicity and God will see only your will to please Him. You may feel cold as ice but that won't lessen God's pleasure toward the act of your will. By the way, Sister, do you think there might be a little self-love present?"

The novice was outraged for a moment. Then, regaining her calm, she looked for a long time at her much-admired friend. It was Teresita's principle to answer the plain truth; she never dressed it up with pretty words. Sister knew that and loved her for it. As she left the infirmary in answer to the call for second table, she smiled at Teresita and said, "You have taught me the meaning of Saint Paul's words, 'I live, now not I, but Christ liveth in me!' "

May was slipping by and Teresita was not improving. On the contrary, severe pains were shooting through her back, her fever was rising, and she suffered loss of appetite. The Community doctor diagnosed her illness as a severe case of bronchitis, and a specialist brought in by her father feared it was developing into pleurisy. An atmosphere of tension and gloom invaded the convent. Long hours of mental prayer were offered by the nuns in petition to Our Lady for a speedy cure.

One morning Doctor Quevedo walked from the infirmary with a heavy step. He had just examined Teresita and, although he tried not to show it, he was worried. Mother Carmen, who waited for him in the corridor, was not at all relieved when he said, "Teresita looks so much like Martha * did in her illness. There is something so angelic about her that I don't know . . . I don't know if God. . . ."

Pretending not to read between the lines and trying to comfort her brother, Mother Carmen suggested: "Since you find pleural disturbances, Calixto, and since you are doubtful about her lungs, do you think it would be a good plan to

* Martha was Dr. Quevedo's sister, who died at the age of twenty.

take her away to the mountains? To a place, perhaps, that would offer more comforts than our infirmary?"

"If she is no better in seventy-two hours after taking this new antibiotic, Carmen, I am going to your Mother Provincial and ask to bring her home." There was a finality in his tone that Mother Carmen knew she must not challenge. Teresita's Lady would solve the problem.

Don Calixto's voice had carried through the open door of the infirmary to the anxious ears of his daughter. Teresita later remarked that she could never explain the feeling that shook her soul "thinking that I might have to leave our beloved novitiate. I had to convince myself that if it should happen it was because Our Lady had ordained it, for that was the only way I could resign myself."

With an unsteady hand she wrote that night in her diary:

Most Holy Mother Mary, I have wanted this month to be one of complete serenity, regardless of the suffering your Divine Son chose to send me. It has been up to now, but I am disturbed thinking that you are going to ask me to leave the novitiate so dear to my heart. I will accept even this with love, peace and generosity if you ask it of me, for I have promised to dispose myself perfectly to your desires. Dearest Mother, you alone know what it will cost me.

The antibiotics were successful, but according to the infirmarian Teresita suffered great pain after those injections. "She never, however, lost her happy disposition nor did the heavenly smile leave her face," said the same Sister. In time, her suffering began to ease and there was a slow recession of pain.

The critical point of the illness had passed when Teresita looked up one afternoon into the face of her aunt, Mother Anita, and said: "I have learned to love our Mother Provincial very much. I suppose it is because I am so grateful that she did not send me from the novitiate when I was critically ill."

"Did you know about that?" Mother Anita asked with surprise.

"Of course, Auntie! I heard Papa telling Tía Carmen in the corridor the day he came to examine me. For days after that, I would waken in the morning wondering if that were to be the day that Reverend Mother would send me home. Those moments were terrifying! But see how God works. . . . He gives strength when and where He wills. Tía Anita, if Reverend Mother had sent me home, I would have died of grief."

"You felt it that keenly, Teresita?"

"Very keenly. It was brought strongly to my mind, at that time, that above all God's gifts I esteem and value my vocation most. You cannot imagine what it costs me to say to Our Lady: 'If I must leave this novitiate I will do so cheerfully in order to give you pleasure.' "

Mother Anita could have remained all evening listening to the expression of the wonderful workings of grace in Teresita's soul, but prudence told her that a long visit would be harmful to her niece. So, with an embrace and a grateful prayer, she left the infirmary, light-hearted indeed, and deeply humbled by that encounter with abandonment.

The Community at Carabanchel began the annual retreat on June second. The master of the spiritual exercises was no other than Father Jesús Quevedo, professor of Theology at the University of Comillas. It was, of course, a mutual joy for Teresita and her uncle. Since she was not able to follow the program of retreat, Father Quevedo used to go to the infirmary to give her the spiritual conferences. Those repeated encounters were undoubtedly ordained by Divine

Providence for the purpose of bringing to light the unknown depths of Teresita's soul.

Early in the retreat Father said to her: "You remember, Teresita, that I was strongly opposed to your entering the convent so young and so unprepared for a life dedicated to teaching, but. . . ."

Her enthusiastic, "But, Tío Jesús, aren't we obliged to give God the very first fruits . . . ." cut into his unfinished sentence.

"Well, yes, if we are sure it is a case of first fruits. You see I know how difficult the life of a Carmelite of Charity is and as I feared. . . ."

She couldn't bear to hear him say it, because it wasn't true that the rigors of the life had made her ill. So again she interrupted, "Oh, yes, Tío, I knew it too; I knew I was not entering to amuse myself playing the piano."

She watched him stifle his reaction. Then he cast his net into new waters, "How did you first become devoted to Our Blessed Mother, Teresita?"

"My devotion to Our Lady goes back to the days of my childhood. Papa taught Luis, Carmen and me to offer our hearts, our souls and our works to the Mother of God every day on awakening. I remember how I used to love the little prayer, 'O my Mother, my Mistress, I offer everything I have to you.' I believe, Tío, that Our Lady herself gave me the devotion."

Every day of the retreat brought new discoveries of the extraordinary beauties of Teresita's soul. Father Quevedo realized that his niece was going to reach spiritual maturity at a very early age. He told Mother Carmen at the close of the retreat, "Teresita impresses me as a person who has received a special grace from Our Blessed Lady, a grace which, according to Saint John of the Cross, few receive. She opened her soul to me during the retreat and I find no trace of human respect in it. Her only anxiety is to know clearly what Our Lady directs her to do in order to please God."

The final injection of streptomycin conquered the stubborn germ, at least for the time, and Sister María Teresa was little by little restored to the common life. Obedience, however, had to be put into play during her period of recuperation, for she always felt well enough to perform some task that was beyond her strength. It was to be expected that she was not equal to the daily Carmelite routine after having spent so much time in bed. Therefore, obedience demanded a common sense comeback, and Teresita was submissive.

Would the attention and care lavished upon Teresita during her illness play havoc with her spiritually? Would she emerge from this period, where she was the center of attraction, spoiled and pampered? There were doubting Thomases who waited to learn the answers to such questions. So we have reason to believe that custody of the eyes was not the most widely practised virtue in the Community when Sister María Teresa returned.

"To the edification of all, Teresita promptly fell back into the pious habits that were such a part of her before she was taken ill. Her silence was admirable, her recollected demeanor, inspiring. She gave beautiful example wherever she went, for she was the living rule of the novitiate," wrote the infirmarian whose charge it was to keep an eye on Sister María Teresa for a few weeks.

For some time after her recuperation Teresita was obliged to say her prayers, to recreate, and to sew in the convent garden because the doctors ordered all the fresh air possible before cold weather set in. Sister Carmen Gonzalez, one of the senior Sisters of the Institute, happened to be visiting in Carabanchel for several days and she noticed the pale novice who spent so much time in the garden. "Who," she asked the Mother Superior, "is the Sister that practically lives in the garden?"

Forgetting about Mother Carmen's novices, the Superior asked, "What Sister?"

"The pale novice, Mother, who always looks as if she is sensibly living in the presence of God?" she replied with utmost sincerity.

"Oh, that is Sister María Teresa of Jesus, Mother Carmen's niece." Mother Superior needed no further description for identification.

If any material object gave joy to Teresita during those long hours in the garden it was a certain little holy card. The Institute has one of its own. It represents Our Blessed Lady seated in a chair, sewing. Her little Son is beside her, leaning against her knee. He is gazing at one of two Carmelite of Charity Sisters, a novice and a professed nun, who, like Our Lady, are sewing. On the veil of the novice Teresita wrote her initials "H.M.T." because she liked to think of herself sewing in such divine company. She always had that card with her when she went to the garden. "It helps me to be recollected," she used to say. "How I hope I will attain the fullness of Our Lady's admonition on the back of the card!" It read: "Imitate me, my child, in all your actions. In sewing, in painting, in studying, in meditating; at prayer, at recreation at meals. Imitate me in your care of the sick, in your attentions to the poor, in your education of youth, or in whatever other occupations you might be employed. In suffering and in joy, let me be the model you try to imitate interiorly and exteriorly. Copy my purity of intention, my charity, my poverty, my mortification and humility, my simplicity and sincerity, my obedience to the divine will, and my uninterrupted love and union with the most Sacred Heart of my Divine Son. This is the spirit of my preferred Institute of Carmelites of Charity to which I have brought you through a special love of my heart so that you may live and die holy. Practice what I have taught you in the novitiate so that the blessing and protection of your Heavenly Mother may never fail you."

Our Blessed Mother's posture on that holy card was erect and dignified, and formerly Teresita had liked to imitate it. However, under a huge oak tree in the garden, Mother Carmen placed a comfortable chair in which Teresita, during her recuperation, was supposed to make her meditation. In fact, she was supposed to rest in that chair whenever she was not strolling among the flowers. One day while making her meditation it occurred to her that she was delightfully comfortable in the chair. "It is time to imitate the posture of the Virgin of my holy card, as I used to before I was taken sick," she thought. So she straightened up, pulled her back away from the chair, and sat with closed eyes, meditating. One of the senior Sisters happened to pass by at that moment. She paused to observe the statue in the chair. "Well," she thought, "you might think she had no other way to mortify herself. As if God hasn't given her enough!"

"Look here, Sister María Teresa," she called, "if Mother Carmen has put that chair out here for you, it is because she wants you to be comfortable. And you can't be unless you rest your back against the cushions."

Teresita bounced back into the chair as if struck by lightning, "Oh yes, Sister. May God reward you!" To Our Lady she whispered: "Thank you, dear Lady, for the occasion to substitute the will of another for my own."

Although quite recovered from the malady, one last precaution was ordered by her father to make sure the pleural cavities were clear. Teresita had to be x-rayed. For this it would be necessary to go to the radiologist's laboratory. Something seemed to cloud her expression when Doctor Quevedo broke the news, but she reserved the question until she was alone with Mother Carmen. "Mother," she said, "if the radiologist asks me to get undressed I will have to tell him no . . . not to bother with the x-ray . . . because to get undressed in his presence is beyond my strength."

Mother Carmen respected her love of modesty but she knew, too, that Teresita needed a little lesson on this point.

"Do not forget, Teresita, that they stripped Christ before His death and He did not whimper. He bowed submissively to the will of His Father. If you refuse anything necessary to the restoration of your good health, you will be denying Our Lady a part of the all you have offered her."

That was May thirty-first. In her diary Teresita wrote:

My dear Mother Mary, your month has ended. With all the gratitude of my heart I thank you for not allowing me to carry out my plan of sacrifice. I know you planned the month for me in conformity with your Divine Son's will. I hope, dear Mother, I have pleased you and in some little way delighted the Divine Heart of Jesus. Please, bless my dear father and all those who shared in my restoration to health! Grant to all who prayed for me an abundance of supernatural grace, for you are the Mediatrix of all graces! And, above all, do not neglect to call on me again, dear Lady, if I can in any way satisfy some tiny portion of Divine Justice!

CHAPTER XV

Teresita's Way of Confidence

ON THE feast of Our Lady of Mount Carmel, 1948, Teresita Quevedo wrote in her diary:

If I thought I were not going to become a saint here, I would have to leave the novitiate. However, since God wants sanctity, nothing less, and since He has brought me to your Carmelite Home, dear Mother Mary, I am completely confident that you will see that I fulfill His will. Every morning at Mass I place the yearning of my heart—my sanctity—in your hands. Thus each day I take one step further toward becoming a saint. For God will take me from your hands and mold me as He wills. I promise you, my Mother, that there will be no stubborn opposition on my part, no matter how difficult the way may become. Dear Lady of Mount Carmel, be my guiding light! Lead me to the perfection that your Son has ordained for me from all eternity! I trust in you blindly, Mother Mary.

Her words are strong; her tone is childlike and confident. There is no doubt about it, Sister María Teresa of Jesus had embraced the life of self-abandonment which is lived by all true children of Our Lady. Hers was a self-abandonment that grows out of an absolute confidence in the Mother of Christ.

Confidence was, of course, the quality that made Teresita's devotion to Our Lady genuine. Let us consider fleetingly the confidence of the little girl who said, "I placed my hand in that of Our Lady as I rose to go to the altar to receive Our Lord on my First Communion Day, because I knew she could give my heart to Jesus better than I." And the confidence of the ten-year-old girl who wrote in her retreat book: "I have decided to become a saint." Then, there is the confidence of the modern, teen-age Teresita who claimed that "people complicate their lives by failing to place their trust in Our Lady." More mature, however, is the confidence of the young lady who told a friend on the eve of her entrance into the convent: "I am confident that I shall become very holy in my new life. You see, Carmen, I have asked Our Lady to make me like herself, and she will deny me nothing that will glorify her Son."

Teresita and a novice friend were chatting in the convent garden one afternoon during recreation period. Like a bolt out of the blue her friend asked: "Teresita, what is the secret of your holiness? I suppose I should not be so blunt. I don't want to embarrass you and you can tell me to 'mind my own holiness' if you wish. However, I would like to know how you go about climbing the ladder of sanctity that leads to union with Christ. Can you share your secret with me?"

Teresita hesitated to answer the Sister because the initial question was so personal. A silent appeal to Our Lady reassured her, and she answered modestly: "Well, you know that sanctity consists in doing all things well; particularly the 'little things' which make up our daily life, Sister. You also know that of ourselves we can do nothing. But, as Saint Paul says, we 'can do all things in Him' who strengthens us.

That is all. I know it well, for of myself I am utterly helpless, Sister. I must keep my hand in that of Our Lady in order to be able to please her Son. Only with my hand in hers can I be confident that I shall reach heaven."

Mother Carmen, who was in the garden cutting flowers, overheard their conversation. She was impressed with Teresita's lack of self-consciousness. Mother knew it was not easy for her niece to rise above the embarrassment the imprudent approach her friend had caused her. She walked toward them.

"May I join you?" Mother surprised them. "I could not help but hear you. Tell me, Sisters, now that you are discussing sanctity, what steps should a novice take in order to become a saint?"

Teresita looked furtively at her aunt and caught the sincerity that deepened the lines of her face. She means it, Teresita thought, but I shall let Sister reply. Her friend, however, shook her head, and Mother's niece was forced to answer.

"Well, Mother," she said, "to become a saint one must take two definite steps: one toward abandonment, the other toward confidence. In other words, one must break all attachments, no matter how holy, and place her soul in Mary's hands, confident that she will offer it to Christ in a manner worthy of Him. Since God will not refuse His Mother anything, He will accept her offering and fashion the soul after His own, which means that it will 'become perfect as our Heavenly Father is perfect.' "

Mother continued: "At times I ask myself how your devotion to Our Lady could be defined, Teresita. Is the keynote 'love for Our Lady' or 'confidence in Our Lady'?"

"You can't divorce one from the other, Madre," was Teresita's immediate response. Confidence grows out of love.

Indeed we can reach any height of perfection if our confidence in the Mother of God is strong enough."

The bell for Vespers brought their conversation to a close.

Sister María Dolores, a classmate of Teresita, was completely down in the depths one day because she could not meditate. Her Rosary was filled with a thousand distractions. Spiritual reading was over before she had begun to concentrate. Apparently, there was nothing right in her spiritual life. Believing herself to be at the brink of despair, she stopped Teresita at the entrance to the novitiate and asked if she could have a word with her.

For twenty minutes Teresita listened to her classmate's self-annihilation. "I can't go on in this miserable state. I'm beginning to hate myself. . . ." she was saying when Teresita broke in.

"There is no reason why you shouldn't hate yourself, María. If you go about it in the right way, you will love God more for hating self," she told her. "Be careful not to let Satan deceive you. It is good for us to recognize our own misery, but when we do, we should be humble, not angry. Perhaps your trouble comes from a lack of confidence in the good God and His Holy Mother. We must have confidence. María. Where would Mary Magdalene have drifted if she had not placed her confidence in Christ? And think of Saint Peter! Would he have become Prince of the Apostles if despair had overcome his confidence? Many times God permits us to see the misery of our soul in order to teach us humility. When we find misery and nothing else in our soul, María, we must offer God that misery. Why don't you do that now?—with confidence in the Sacred Hearts of Jesus and Mary! If you embrace a way of confidence, María, you will never again suffer the depression that dwells in your soul today."

"God reward you, Teresita!" Without further talk, Sister María Dolores turned from the novitiate and walked toward the chapel.

When Teresita went to her cell that evening, she found a holy card of Our Lady of Mount Carmel on her desk. Turning it over, she read: "You have taught me confidence today. Pray that I may never lose it. Your devoted H.M.D."

Mother Carmen tells us that Teresita's close associates at the novitiate had learned that Sister María Teresa always suffered some small trial on a feast day of Our Lady. "It was a painful humiliation, a mortification, a physical ailment, or some other splinter of the Cross," Mother says. "The pattern followed a fixed design."

One day Teresita, who usually confided such thoughts only to her diary, said to Mother Carmen: "I am beginning to anticipate Our Lady's feasts with a kind of fear, Madre. I know she will prick me with thorns as she scatters roses on the other novices."

Teresita had been watering the red geraniums in the novitiate window boxes as she was speaking to Mother Carmen. They had lapsed into silence. Teresita looked up and found her aunt's gaze intently fixed upon her. Mother quickly picked up the thread of their conversation.

"You were saying, Teresita, that you are getting to dislike the pin-pricks that the Blessed Mother sends you on her feast days."

"No, Madre, not 'dislike'; I really welcome them. When I said I anticipate her feasts with a kind of fear, I meant a fear of not measuring up to what Our Lady expects of me on those occasions."

"How do you handle those fears, Sister?" Mother asked.

"Well, Madre, by what I call my *caminito de confianza.*"

"Your 'little way of confidence'? What is that, Teresita?"

"It is an utter trust in Our Lady, Madre. It is being confident that all things—even those pin-pricks—come to us from our Holy Mother for our sanctification. Whenever I begin my meditation, mental prayer, office, or any other spiritual exercise, I unite my soul with Mary's and I say to her: 'Virgin Mother of God, your weak child begs you to turn her distractions into your own holy thoughts. I place all my confidence in you!' Then I go on with my prayer because I am confident that, if I fail, my Mother will take over. Thus God will be praised every moment."

"Indeed He will be praised every moment. Do you confine this 'little way of confidence,' as you call it, to spiritual duties?"

"Oh, no, Madre! I try to approach everything in that way. Before starting on any of my assigned duties I say: 'Dearest Mother, will you please supply whatever I lack in order to do this work perfectly.' "

"And does she, Teresita?"

"I am absolutely confident that she does, Madre. No matter how small or insignificant a petition may be, regardless of how great it may be, confidence has a way of reaching the depths of Our Lady's heart. She cannot resist its urge to induce her Divine Son to be indulgent toward her confident children."

A year after Teresita's death, in 1951, Father Muzquiz told the novices at Carabanchel that her "way of confidence" was built on the queen of virtues—humility. He encouraged them to imitate it because it is within the grasp of any sincere child of Mary. As Teresita did, they would have to lay a foundation for their confidence; otherwise Our Lady could construct only a toppling spiritual edifice in the soul. To dig a deep foundation, they would have to use a sharp and strong implement. Certainly not the spade of self-reliance. Teresita's spade was that of self-knowledge—complete self-knowledge, he told them. And, in her own words, Father showed them this perfect picture Teresita had painted of her "self":

Teresita knew her own nothingness:

> I am nothing, dear Lady, nothing but a wormy apple (she wrote). Will you, my Mother, pare this apple and feed it to your Son—a little at a time. As you prepare each portion, I know you will cut away the wormy spots and feed Him only the sweet meat. In that way, my Jesus will enjoy His little apple and when the last portion is consumed, my nothingness will be lost in Him.

Teresita felt her weakness:

> How weak I am, dear Mother of God! My defects are numerous, yet you never weary of me. That is why I am not alarmed when I see myself filled with faults. However, dear Lady, I am completely aware that my weakness is the reason why you take me by the hand. If you did not, I would stumble and fall! Dear Mother, my weakness makes me understand that I can do nothing without you (she wrote in her diary during her first illness).

Of her misery she says:

> Sweet Lady, I am misery itself, holding strongly to your mantle of blue! If I were less miserable, you would not protect and care for me as you do. Since my misery keeps me small and very much in need of your sweet attentions, I do not regret being a miserable soul.

Teresita's helplessness was clear to her. In her diary we find:

I expect nothing from myself because I am as helpless as a new-born babe. But I expect everything from you, dear Mother Mary—even sanctity, which of myself I cannot reach.

"That is how Teresita dug her foundation with the spade of self-knowledge. That is why humility, the queen of virtues, is the base of her confidence in Our Lady," Father explained to the young nuns who had seen Teresita follow her "little way of confidence."

As Sister Maria Teresa's confidence grew, it revealed a number of strong qualities. Outstanding is the "incomparable purity" of her confidence. Hers was not a mixture of confidence in Our Lady and confidence in self—the confidence which pervades the little spiritual world of many souls who serve Our Lady less perfectly than she. Pure confidence such as Teresita's never wavers! Her Superiors say they never knew her confidence to falter, for "she was as radiant when desolation wracked her soul as she was when her life was serene with consolation and joy."

During her illness, an elderly member of the Community asked Teresita: "Why are you so sure Our Lady is going to take you to Heaven?"

"Because," she answered, "I have perfect confidence in my Mother. She knows how her daughter is longing to look at the radiant beauty of her Mother's face, and to listen to the sweetness of her voice, and to delight in a closeness to her she has never known here on earth."

The most beautiful melody in Teresita's medley of confidence is the one we have heard her sing so frequently in her diary—her childlike confidence. She writes, for example, of having been spoiled by Our Lady: "Dearest Mother, with all your goodness, you pamper me anew every day. Only my sanctity can repay you! Will you make me a saint? I cannot merit sanctity myself but you can merit it for me, since you are my Mother. I want to be a saint so that I will resemble you more closely and, consequently, win more abundantly the love of your Son."

There is a strong childlike confidence in the following letter that Teresita wrote to the Blessed Virgin when she was a postulant.

Dearest Mother Mary: Today one of the Sisters asked me how I could say I hoped to become a saint. I answered her: 'I do not say it boastfully as you seem to infer, Sister. I say it because I am confident that my Holy Mother wants to make a saint of her poor, weak child who of herself will never be worth a fig. Our Lady awakened the desire of sanctity in me on my First Communion day. She did it, undoubtedly, because her Son wills me to aspire to sanctity. I have always hoped to become a saint in the same way my brother Luis has always wanted to become an engineer. I know, of course, that I am as far removed from God's glorious saints as the dandelion is from the orchid. That does not discourage me. Don't you think, Sister, that Luis would be wrong if he should say that he is not going to follow his engineering career because Mr. So-and-So is such an eminent engineer, and that he must not aspire to the heights of a Mr. So-and-So? If men reasoned like that, we would have no future engineers, doctors, lawyers. So, Sister, neither am I going to say that I cannot become a saint because Teresa of Avila was a great mystic and far beyond my mettle. That would be an absurd lack of confidence in the dearest of Mothers. It is much better to leave sanctity in the hands of a Provident Father who will sanctify whom He will. All my trust is in Mary and she will bring it to her Son for me.' Dearest Mother, I must always be aware of this truth—I am your child, wholly your child."

"Teresita's confidence was utter love," Mother Carmen told Father Muzquiz as she handed him a letter. "Read this,

Father; it is a little gem of spiritual advice that she wrote to her sister Carmen."

Father knew that Carmen was being courted by a young man named Javier. He knew about the mental depressions into which Carmen lapsed after Teresita entered the convent. He knew they had returned again, whenever Javier's business took him out of town for weeks at a time. Therefore, Father readily followed the letter Mother handed him. It read:

Dearest *Chatina:* When I received your second letter I was amazed because I was not expecting it. . . .

It pains me to know that you feel the need of so many attentions to keep you happy, *Chatina,* . . . Your letters tell me that you had a wonderful time while Javier was in town. Can't you use those blissful memories as a prop during the weeks he is away?

Now that you are alone and have time to think, I am going to talk to you frankly—as I would if you were here beside me. Everyone who loves God ought to know that nothing can fill the human heart but His divine love. No one can completely satisfy our heart's longings but God. I was reading some excerpts from Saint Augustine recently and this one is for you, Carmen: 'Our hearts were made for God and they will not rest until they rest in Him!' How wise Augustine was! Please, say it over and over again when you grow restless. It will calm you!

Do not think for a moment, *Chatina,* that we can love without suffering. Perhaps you will say that I do not understand my dear *Chatina's* sufferings. Indeed, I understand them perfectly. My religious clothing has not snatched my human nature from me. I know what longing for love is even more acutely than you. For when Christ abandons me, there is only my own misery left in my soul—God takes Our Lady with Him! When Javier leaves you there is the natural human void, but Everything remains in your heart because Christ does not travel off with Javier. Moreover, 'hope' resides in your knowledge of the time of his return.

My dearest *Chatina,* if you let Him, Christ will teach you that there is joy in suffering. When you understand this, you will realize that suffering is one of God's greatest gifts to us. Suffering is the gift that brings us closest to the heart of Christ. Suffering is love. If it weren't, *Chatina,* do you think God the Father would have sent His Son on earth to suffer?

What you need is a strong and loving confidence in Mary. Pray for it! I shall ask my dearest Mother to take mine and place it in your heart, *Chatina.* I can toddle along without it for awhile, since my hand is fairly glued to that of my Mother. . . .

CHAPTER XVI

Holy Year

ONE evening at recreation, during Advent 1949, the novices were commenting enthusiastically on the Holy Year preparations being made in Rome. Of chief interest was the proclamation disclosing the Holy Father's decision to declare the Assumption of the Blessed Virgin Mary a dogma of faith before the close of 1950. Sister María Teresa had no intention of changing the theme of their conversation, but without realizing that she was doing so, she fairly shouted: "Sisters, I am sure Our Lady is going to grant me a very unique privilege!"

The element of mystery in her comment and the satisfaction that masked her face brought on a deluge of questions.

"What is it?" questioned Sister Jacinta.

"Tell us what you mean, Sister!" asked Sister Guadalupe.

"What is Our Lady going to give you?" begged Sister María Prieto.

"Will it be a privilege for the entire Community?" This came from Mother Carmen.

"I cannot tell you," Teresita answered. "If it shouldn't happen, you will accuse me of building castles in the air. If it should, then you might forever after call me a soothsayer," she smiled.

Curious novices are not easily defeated. Teresita was forced to relent. "Since there will be a new dogma in honor of one of Our Lady's prerogatives declared this year, there are certain privileges bound to be extended by Our Lady to her little exiles here on earth," she said. "Something tells me that one of those privileges will be mine. Sisters, I believe I am going to celebrate the new dogma in heaven."

Protests galore filled the novitiate. Some laughed; no one took her seriously. Yet with strong conviction she continued: "Go on, *Hermanitas,* laugh at me. But remember what they say about the one who laughs last! Every one of you will probably sing my requiem before the close of 1950. I know I shall be with my Mother on her glorious day. Can you imagine, Sisters, what Heaven will be like when the dogma of the Assumption is declared!"

Apprehension shook the calm of Mother Carmen's heart. But she turned toward her niece and commented jovially: "Before you make reservations for that flight to heaven, my dear little Sister, there is a retreat debt to be settled with Our Lord."

Sister María Teresa had been too weak in July to make the ten-day Community retreat. She and another novice who also had been ill were now about to embark on a private one. Those two *palomitas,** as Reverend Mother called them, would have no priestly direction on their retreat. Mother

* Little doves.

Carmen would be "retreat master." This duty she would have to carry out sporadically, however, because of the other numerous demands upon her attention throughout the day.

Teresita and her companion were finally isolated. No recreation. No classes. Their solitude released them from the tasks they daily performed about the convent. That left plenty of time for prayer, meditation and spiritual reading over and above the daily spiritual exercises of a Carmelite Sister of Charity. They were compelled to keep unbroken silence and to stay apart from the Community, for "Non in commotione Dominus," Mother Carmen told them.

If her former school companions could have watched the order of Teresita's ten-day isolation, comments of "How boring!" "How can she stand it?" would unquestionably have been heard. To Sister María Teresa it was a foretaste of eternity. Every free hour found her before the Blessed Sacrament, absorbed in prayer, or kneeling before the statue of Our Lady.

Teresita entered her private retreat with determination. She was prepared to show Our Lord and His Blessed Mother her spirit of courage and generosity. On September third she wrote:

> I am beginning this retreat resolved to make a good one because I need it. I am prepared to be completely generous with God. I must set right the weak spiritual state of my soul with the help of my Mother Mary. Make me see your holy will clearly, my Jesus, and do not permit my poor dispositions to prevent me from receiving the many graces You are prepared to give me during the coming days of solitude and prayer. Most Holy Virgin, you are my Mother, do not abandon me. Do not permit any fault of mine to keep the grace of Jesus from entering my soul. In you, O Spouse of Joseph, I place my hope to please Jesus.

That was the only entry in her spirtual diary until the night retreat closed, when she wrote:

> The retreat went very well. How constantly I felt the protection of Our Lady! I have given myself to God unreservedly. I expect nothing from Him in return except the privilege of being completely united with my Mother Mary in Him.

Plenty of rest . . . longer recreation periods . . . the rare gift of free time. Those are the things that ease the Rule at Carabanchel from Christmas Eve until after the feast of the Epiphany. That departure from the strict order of convent life is a sound practice. Not only does it revitalize the body and soul of the novice but also those of the Mistress who cares for and directs her throughout the year.

The holy festivities of Christmas begin on the eve, with High Mass at midnight. A breakfast follows, flavored with delicacies unusual in convent fare. Immediately afterwards, the novices make their first visit to the Crib in the novitiate. Kneeling in a semi-circle around the image of the new-born King, each Sister welcomes Him by reciting a poem of her own composition. For the gifted member it is merely another opportunity to sing her deep love and devotion to the Divine Child. For the timid and prosaic novice it constitutes an act of virtue almost beyond her power to perform. For the professed Sister looking on, it is an inspiring moment which carries her back to former Christmases.

On the Christmas Eve of Holy Year, Mother Carmen's novices were gathered for the welcome ceremony to the Infant King. Following the order of seniority, each read her poem kneeling before the Crib in the spruce-bedecked novitiate aglow with candle light. A soft but resonant voice told Mother Carmen that Teresita was reciting her humble ballad of love.

During this Holy Year
I desire to cull,
From Sanctity's garden
My Lady's sweet love. . . .

it began. Teresita's theme never varied. An expression of love for Our Lady seemed to be the perfect prelude for her welcome to Jesus.

When that ceremony ended, the novices turned to another appealing Christmas custom of the Carmelite Sisters of Charity. They refer to it as the Christmas *cartitas*—little letters or notes. During Advent, the Mistress of Novices writes a spiritual message for as many Sisters as there are in the novitiate. She seals them, and on Christmas Eve she tucks the nameless envelopes among the greens that bank the Christ Child's Crib. It is a traditional belief among the young nuns that each *cartita* will reach the Sister for whom its message is intended. Nevertheless, a casual observer could see that there were skeptics in Sister María Teresa's group. Several novices fingered various envelopes before selecting the one that "felt" as if it held a message for her. When their selections were made, they opened and reverently read the spiritual tid-bit. A stream of emotion filled the room with the same quiet effect as a rainbow arching itself against the sky.

"Live very closely united to My Mother so that she may teach you to give Me pleasure in all that you do" was the content of the *cartita* that Teresita received when she was a postulant. This Holy Year message was more complex. It read: "In order to attain the perfection to which you are obliged, do not forget that the essential point resides in constancy and perseverance in the vocation you have embraced. Your exterior life and surroundings need not be an enemy to your interior life, since all you do should be directed toward Me."

Teresita, carrying that message in her heart, continued to be the same gracious person exteriorly, but she was changing profoundly in her soul. She worked with might and main to reach "the perfection to which she was obliged." As a result, her ideals became so lofty that she could not find satisfaction in anything except what brought her directly to a closer union with God. If obedience ordered it, then the diversions and innocent pleasures of a novice were the fine gold of God's holy will. When the choice was left to her, she chose one of her great ideals: mortification, charity, or humility. In them she rejoiced a thousand times more than she could have in the most delightful of innocent pleasures. Everyone in the novitiate did not understand that; but the book of perfection is like a book of mathematics: there are problems in it that are not meant to be solved by everyone.

On New Year's Day, 1950, Sister María Teresa sent a letter to her Aunt and Uncle.

My dearest *Tiucus* (she wrote), since Reverend Mother is going to write you, I have taken advantage of the opportunity to enclose a note in which I send you my deep affection and many wishes for a New Year filled with spiritual blessings which, thank God, are the only blessings that count.

1950 promises to be a completely happy year, for I shall make my vows, God willing. I want to make the most of my preparation for this great act of immolation, because I intend to give myself unconditionally to God, with the help of my Mother Mary.

Pray that each day of 1950 will find me more worthy of becoming a spouse of Christ. As my novitiate days draw to a close, I clearly see the shallowness of my virtue, and it frightens me. The only comfort I have is the knowledge that Mary will never abandon me. She takes more care of her weak children than of her stronger ones who need less help. *Tiucos,* I must become a saint.

Love to cousin Dolores. My affection and abundant prayers for all of you.

María Teresa of Jesus, Carmelite Novice of Charity.

The following day, January second, three of Teresita's school chums visited her. She warmly greeted them, graciously entertained them with light chatter and hearty laughter, but later one of the girls said: "She did seem far away in spite of her amiability."

When the girls rose to leave that afternoon, Teresita gave a light tone of authority to words which made a deep impression on the girls. "Go to Mass and Communion often, girls; try to say the Rosary every day and, above all, increase your love for Our Blessed Lady," she said as she waved them *adiós.*

"What precisely are the characteristics that mark the spirituality of your niece, Father?" a renowned bishop asked Father Jesús Quevedo, S.J., in January of 1950.

Teresita's uncle was rather surprised that the bishop should bring up such a serious topic in the midst of a reception being held to honor a venerable Jesuit jubilarian in Madrid. Father Quevedo turned from his appetizer to answer: "Ordinarily I have little to say about Teresita, as Your Excellency knows, but since you ask, I must say that I believe Teresita's virtue is genuine. It has nothing theatrical about it. She strikes me as being a truly simple soul, sincere and humble. Simplicity certainly is her outstanding characteristic. I would say, too, that her life is one great desire to please the Blessed Virgin in every way she possibly can, and that her confidence in Our Lady far exceeds that of an ordinary soul. In saying this,

Your Excellency, I hope that none of the prejudices of flesh and blood have entered into my judgment."

The bishop made no comment, but Father Quevedo was not surprised at that.

A week after that event, the bishop had occasion to visit Carabanchel. He asked the identical question of Sister María Teresa's superiors. Her Postulant Mistress, Sister María, was the first to reply: "I can best describe Teresita Quevedo as a recollected soul. Moreover, she is one who does the little things in life exceptionally well. It is a perfection in little things that makes her different from the usual novice. And although she never does anything extraordinary, she herself is extraordinary. I hope I make myself clear, Your Excellency."

Sister María's appraisal of a soul was confirmed by the other Council members. Reverend Mother added: "We must not forget to stress the fact that Sister María Teresa has become a Carmelite only in order to become a saint, Your Excellency. Her personal sanctification was the only reason she gave when I asked her why she wanted to become a Religious. Shortly after she entered the novitiate, I could see that a desire for holiness and for the perfection of little things obsessed her. I can still see her, a postulant of one month, binding a book in the novitiate bookshop. What assiduous care she took to do a perfect job! When she became aware of my interest in her work, she said, 'I am a little slow, Reverend Mother. It is better, however, to finish the binding a little later and to have it done as perfectly as possible, isn't it?' Her norm was perfection."

"I can add to Teresita's perfection in little things, Your Excellency," offered Mother Carmen. "You know something of her background, so you understand that domestic chores are not her forte. It amuses me to see her tidy up the refectory or scour the pots and pans in the kitchen when she is on duty there. And I shall never forget the first day I assigned her to the laundry. It seemed cruel, with her lack of experience, to send her right off to the washtubs, but I did. She was clumsy and she knew it. However, she would not be conquered by a rubbing board. I stood in the background watching her as she approached the Sister in charge of the laundry. '*Hermana,*' she said, 'I want to wash the toques well, but I'm afraid I don't know how. Will you watch my method for a while and tell me how to improve it?' I knew then that Teresita needed very little help from me. Good common sense and humility were her guiding stars."

"Your Excellency, just listen to this," Reverend Mother broke in again. "One very warm day in September I passed through the pressing room and found our little Sister hard at work, cleaning and pressing her habit. I commented on her vanity in always wanting to look nice. She turned off the iron, knelt at my feet and stunned me with her reply: 'May God and Our Lady forgive me if I am vain, Reverend Mother! May I have a penance?' A little surprised, I nodded for her to rise. She went on: 'I know I like to wear clean and well-pressed clothes, Reverend Mother. Mama saw to it that neatness was ingrained in all of us from childhood. I have never looked upon it as vanity. . . . But, Mother, if wives in the world go to such extremes to look beautiful in the eyes of their husbands, don't you think we, spouses of a Divine Bridegroom, should dress in keeping with the dignity that is ours? Poverty does not oppose cleanliness, does it, Reverend Mother?' What could I answer except: Go in peace, my child!"

"And that, Reverend Mother, is what I shall do immediately," said the good bishop, rising and elevating his right hand in benediction over the three nuns.

CHAPTER XVII

Profession

On January 18, 1950, Sister María Teresa told Mother Carmen that she had a very severe headache.

"How long have you had it, Sister?"

"Since yesterday morning, Mother," Teresita replied.

"Why didn't you mention it before?"

"Because it came upon me suddenly, Mother, and I expected it to pass over. Those sudden headaches usually do."

A number of novices were ill with the grippe, and Mother thought Teresita was just one more. She sent her to the infirmary, where the nurse gave her the remedy the doctor had prescribed for the others. Teresita went off to bed for the day, fully convinced that the medicine would nip her cold in the bud, as the infirmarian had said.

On the nineteenth Teresita seemed well—perfectly normal, in fact, and she went about her daily tasks with characteristic care.

Late in the afternoon Mother Carmen called her to the novitiate.

"How do you feel, Sister?" she asked.

"The headache is no better, Mother; in fact, it gets worse when I walk. My back aches, too." She forced a smile. Teresita did not want to displease Our Lord by gloomily airing her pain.

"Well, since it is so close to Angelus, Sister, take supper with us in the refectory. Afterwards, ask the infirmarian for another cold capsule and go directly to bed." And Mother Carmen, so extremely solicitous toward the other sick novices, forgot to tell her niece to stay in bed on the following morning until the late Mass.

Teresita rose at the first stroke of the bell on the morning of the twentieth. Meditation and Mass presented no problem, and breakfast was not the ordeal she had anticipated. She felt able to navigate, in fact, until grace after breakfast had been said. Then Mother Carmen rang the little silver bell for attention. Directing herself to the novices, she said, "Sisters, I would like you to reflect on the way in which Sister María Teresa of Jesus interprets our holy customs. I thought you all knew by this time that when a Sister is sent to retire early, she is *ipso facto* to remain in bed the following day until the students' Mass." Mother paused.

No one stirred. Eyes were cast down. A flushed face could be seen here and there. How could Mother Mistress humiliate their Teresita like this? But somehow they were reminded that: "Whom He loveth, He chastiseth." That soothed the sting.

Momentarily Teresita forgot to keep absolute custody of the eyes. Looking up at her beloved aunt, she blushed, then smiled. She quivered a bit as she knelt to ask for a penance. Mother beckoned her to rise, for she read an expression of deep pain in Teresita's eyes. She did not know, however, whether to attribute it to a severe headache or to the rebuke her niece had suffered. Acting in favor of the former, Mother waived the public penance that ordinarily follows such breaches of the customs.

Teresita took her place on the long white line that moved from the refectory to the chapel. There was no indication of her severe physical pain, nor the wound that humility had just inflicted upon her. To be sure, Sister María Teresa of Jesus had learned to conquer self.

Office. Rosary. Spiritual reading. Recreation. Study. Teresita had followed the horarium of the day without dispensation until five o'clock in the afternoon. Her last class ended, she turned to Sister María Guadalupe and asked her to gather up her books and put them in her desk in the novitiate. "I am very ill," she told her. "I cannot manage to do it myself. Thank you, Sister Guadalupe."

Mother Carmen sent her niece to the infirmary. It was the vigil of Saint Agnes' feast and, as she prepared for bed, Teresita could hear the Community chanting the office for the feast. Before retiring, she knelt heavily on the floor, leaned her head on the edge of the mattress and followed Agnes in her heart. "How beautiful the verses were! 'I come to You whom I have loved, whom I have sought and whom I have desired.... You loved justice and abhorred iniquity: therefore God, your God, has anointed you with His holy oil, preferring you to your companions.... Be happy with me and rejoice with me because from all the suffering that He has visited upon me, I have received the crown of eternal glory.... Jesus, Spouse of virgins, Son of the Virgin Mary, who has brought you up among the lilies ... who has poured grace on your lips ... has blessed you from all eternity.' "

Early the following morning, January twenty-first, Mother Carmen called her brother on the telephone. "Hello, Calixto," she said, "I wish I didn't have to tell you this. Teresita's headaches through the night have been severe. This morning she has a slight rise in temperature and complains of stiffness in her back."

An anxious frown passed over Doctor Quevedo's forehead as he told his sister he would be at the novitiate within the hour.

"Hello, Teresita! What are you doing in bed again?" teased her father as he entered the infirmary.

Could this happy child be gravely ill, he thought as she answered, "Yes, Papa. Saint Agnes has put me here this time."

He gave his daughter a thorough examination. Then followed a brief visit and an affectionate farewell. Exteriorly he appeared her happy, jesting father. Interiorly he was an anguished, doubtful man.

Mother Carmen and other members of the Council paced the corridor outside the infirmary awaiting his diagnosis.

"I am afraid Teresita will not be with us long," he bravely admitted to them. "I believe she has tuberculous meningitis. All of the symptoms are not clearly discernible as yet but I know they will be after we make a few laboratory tests. Reverend Mother, you must call in your Community doctor, but do not mention my diagnosis to him. He knows the history of her illness last May. Dr. Lozano is an excellent physician and will give my child the best of care. Let me know the result of his visit."

Doctor Lozano arrived shortly after receiving Mother Superior's call. His step was not as quick as usual when he left the infirmary, so Reverend Mother was not surprised when he said: "She seems to have the symptoms of tuberculous meningitis, Reverend Mother, but I should like to hold off telling her good father until I am absolutely certain. Good day, Sisters, I'll call you when the laboratory tests come through."

The Doctor did not know that Dr. Quevedo was waiting at Dr. Lozano's office to exchange with him the findings of the morning examinations.

"Calixto, why are you so positive that nothing can be done for Teresita?" Dr. Lozano tried to be optimistic, but his sincere friendship for his colleague would not allow him to phrase his words in any but interrogative fashion.

Every line in Dr. Quevedo's handsome face spelled desolation. "If you can suggest any category other than terminal into which we may put our findings, Lozano, I'll be the happiest man alive," he answered.

"There is always the possibility of error, Calixto. Let us file our diagnoses and call Dr. Marañon in to make another." Dr. Lozano sounded hopeful. Dr. Marañon was reputed to be one of the best diagnosticians in Western Europe and happened to be a friend of Dr. Quevedo.

"There is no other diagnosis, and you know it," he replied with finality.

Teresita's case was indeed hopeless. Dr. Quevedo was sure he would have to bring her home because she had not yet made the vows. Strange, he thought, how he felt about it now. A year ago he wanted nothing more than to bring her back to the comforts of her home and the loving care of her mother. Dr. Quevedo braced himself, dialed the number of the Mother Provincial of the Carmelite Sisters of Charity and asked for an appointment with Reverend Mother. "Yes, Reverend Mother is here," the secretary told him, "and she will be happy to see you this afternoon at four."

Seated opposite Reverend Mother Dolores Castell, Doctor Quevedo stated his case: "I understand, Mother, that Teresita's terminal illness means that she will have to leave the novitiate. Mother, my daughter will die in a matter of months no matter where she is. The best of care can not prevent it. Her case is not one of lifetime paralysis. Dr. Lozano and I are positive that a period of agony is not far off and that it will be an immediate prelude to her death, Mother. As I was saying. . . ."

"Please do not take Teresita from our novitiate, Doctor," Reverend Mother Dolores interrupted. "We know what blessings her presence here has brought and will continue to bring to the Community. We shall feel privileged to care for her as long as Our Lord ordains and we shall spare nothing in an effort to save your child. She could not be happy outside the house of God and it would be cruel to allow anything to disturb the tranquillity of her soul. Doctor, please allow us to take care of Teresita until God calls her."

"Thank you, Reverend Mother. Your generosity is more than I would dare to hope for. My dear child will die happier in God's house. . . ." Don Calixto lowered his head. As he did, the image of his princess that he carried in his heart comforted him. He rose and took leave of Mother Dolores with warm gratitude.

The news of Sister María Teresa's grave illness spread quickly through the Community, the Academy, and even through the city, where her father was highly respected. Distressed novices, sad academy friends, stunned professed Sisters, all petitioned Heaven for a miracle.

"I don't know how this spiritual battle is going to end," Mother Dolores Castell said to Dr. Quevedo one day in the infirmary. "Everyone, except Teresita, is praying for a miracle. Your child must have tremendous power in Heaven, however, for God seems to be drawing her closer to eternity every day."

Teresita listened as Mother spoke to her father, but she did not comment. On her face there was an expression of joy and a knowledge superior to theirs.

There was no imminent danger of death, but the doctors feared that Teresita might lose her mental faculties without warning. Doctor Quevedo, therefore, advised Mother Carmen to have her anointed. Preparations were made and Mother Carmen gave her father the joy of breaking this news to her. It was January twenty-fourth, feast of Our Lady of Peace. Don Calixto bent over his daughter's bed and began: "My child, you are very, very ill. Mother Carmen has asked me to tell you...."

A tight squeeze of his hand and a new light in Teresita's eyes indicated that she knew what he was about to suggest and desired it with all her heart.

To be absolutely certain, Dr. Quevedo went on: "You know, dear, what a precious treasure the Church offers her critically ill children. Do you remember how quickly I recovered after receiving Extreme Unction?"

"Oh, yes, Papa." Her voice sounded strong. "There is nothing I should like more than to receive the Last Sacraments."

"God bless my princess," he answered. "Now, Teresita, as a holy preface to your anointing, Reverend Mother has a surprise for you. It will increase your happiness as nothing else could." Don Calixto stepped aside to make room for Reverend Mother Dolores Castell.

Mother Dolores smiled affectionately at the little novice. "Sister María Teresa of Jesus," she told her, "you are going to make your Holy Vows today. You will then be a Professed Sister, a true Carmelite of Charity, and you will enjoy all the privileges our state in life offers to those who are about to appear before their Creator."

The expression on Sister María Teresa's face was sublime, but she did not put her interior emotion into words. She answered simply: "May God reward you, dear Reverend

Mother!" Brevity in speech on matters regarding herself had always been characteristic of Teresita. It prompted the Mother Bursar who witnessed this scene to turn to the nurse and comment: "Sister María Teresa has always had so much to say to Our Lady and so little to say to us."

The infirmarian's reply was perfect. "Sister's reserve, Mother, springs from her desire to be considered nothing in the eyes of people. She longed for the love of God and His Mother and she never ceased to tell them so."

Teresita watched Sister Jacinta's experienced hands arrange the table with the requisites for the Sacrament she was about to receive. The nurse was so quiet Teresita wondered if she were ill. Or did she see a trace of sadness in her nurse's expression?

"Come here, Sister Jacinta, I want to tell you something before I begin my prayer," Teresita whispered. The nurse took her patient's hand. "I want to tell you how happy I am today and how very much I feel Our Lady's presence near me," she told her.

"Don't you feel a bit sad when you think of leaving all you love, Teresita?"

"Why should I, Sister? I am not leaving all I love. I have a Father in Heaven who is waiting for me and a Mother who will come here to bring me to Him. I have always loved Our Lady above everything and everyone; that is my greatest comfort now. Sister Jacinta, if you would but love Our Lady with your whole heart—with every fiber of your being—you would never suffer sadness, not even while looking death straight in the face."

"Teresita, I know—everyone here knows—that you have won an extraordinary love of Our Lady. How have you done it?"

"Only by trying to do the little things in life with perfection. I have never done anything great. What I have done, I have done for God through Mary. My attentions to her have been little ones, *Hermanita*. I have won her, I suppose, because it is the little things that count, and I have won Jesus through Mary."

Teresita received the Last Sacraments and passed the remainder of the day absolutely free from pain. It seemed as if Our Lord had given her relief so that she could prepare herself unreservedly for Profession. "She was completely absorbed with her 're-baptism,' as she referred to it," Mother Carmen said. "I found her so well after lunch that I suggested she write a letter to her Jesuit uncles to tell them the good news. She replied, however, that she preferred to spend the time preparing for her Profession. She promised to write them later. 'Speak to me about the vows, Madre,' she pleaded. I sat down and spoke to her of the grandeur of Holy Profession and of our unworthiness to receive the vows. In conclusion I asked her if she felt she had yet earned Heaven."

"Heaven? Oh, no, Madre, I have not earned it. Jesus and Mary are giving it to me. You know the story of the Good Thief! Since I have never deliberately separated myself from God and His Mother, they are going to seal my union with them now in this wondrous gift of Profession. They are the Master and Mistress of Heaven, you know, and I am their little servant. O Madre, how strongly they have shown me their love! Our Lord is giving me Heaven through Our Lady."

The Community thought it would please Teresita to have her director, Father Muzquiz, officiate at her private Profession ceremony. He in turn invited Teresita's father, for a doctor may visit the sick at any hour according to the Rule of the Institute. Toward five o'clock in the afternoon they arrived together at Carabanchel. Father Muzquiz went into the sick room alone in order to hear Teresita's confession.

"God reward you," she said when he finished. "All day I have been dwelling on God's mercy, Padre. How good Our Lady has been to me! As soon as I get to Heaven, I shall take a place at her side. At last I know that nothing will ever again separate me from Jesus and His adorable Mother!"

At six o'clock the entire Community at Carabanchel, including three Reverend Mothers from the Generalate who had come to attend the Profession ceremony of Teresita, gathered at the foot of the long staircase that led to the second story where the infirmary was located. The priest, carrying the Blessed Sacrament, preceded by two Sisters with lighted candles, followed the long line of black and white veils that slowly and with dignity ascended the broad stairs.

The momentary emotion and the thought of the novice who was waiting above gave a new accent to the verses of the Miserere: "Wash me and I shall be made whiter than snow.... You who loved the truth.... You will speak to me words of comfort and joy.... O God, my God, a humble heart you will not despise.... You will accept the sacrifices of justice." It was indeed a moving spectacle to contemplate so many souls consecrated to God, moving in unison toward a scene that was to enact the fulfillment of Christ's divine promise: "If anyone loves Me, My Father will love him and I will love him and will manifest Myself to him."

The holy silence was broken only by the calm, joyous voice of Teresita. Her eyes were fastened in ecstatic union on the Sacred Host the priest held before her: "I, Sister María Teresa Quevedo y Cadarso, of Jesus, do vow and promise to God Poverty, Chastity and Obedience, according to the Constitutions of the Institute of the Carmelite Sisters of Charity."

Reverend Mother Visitation, Vicaress General, who had remained at the head of Teresita's bed for the ceremony, answered in the name of the absent Superior General: "I admit you into the participation of all the merits and privileges of the Institute, of its indulgences and spiritual favors which come from the Apostolic concessions or from the union of all the meritorious works performed by the members of the Institute. In the name of the Father, and of the Son, and of the Holy Ghost."

Father Muzquiz, visibly moved, recommended Teresita to offer the sacrifice of her life and all the suffering that she was to endure in the future for Pope Pius XII's Holy Year intentions.

"That should make me Our Holy Father's special child," she said as she lifted her head, having finished her act of immolation.

From her bed Teresita followed the Benediction in chapel below, which closed her Profession ceremony. As the Sisters' choir sang the "Tota Pulchra Es, Maria," she closed her eyes and whispered audibly: "My Beloved to me, and I to my Beloved."

Mother Visitation sat closely observing the new little spouse of Christ. "For a long time," Mother said, "she remained with closed eyes and with an unforgettable expression of rapture on her face. There are no words to express what I saw in her. It was something holy and undefinable that reminded me of the virgins Agnes, Cecilia and Thérèse."

Doctor Quevedo had not moved from the place at the side of his daughter's bed to which Mother Superior had led him before the ceremony. Looking at his strong face, Mother thought that he, too, seemed absorbed in contemplation. This had been a moment of supreme grace for him and, although he was grief-stricken, he knew that it would be nothing short of wretched ingratitude to try to prevent Teresita's flight to Heaven.

It was growing dark. Sister Teresa, the aunt who had nurtured Teresita's devotion to Our Lady in her Academy days, tiptoed into the infirmary to say farewell. Her niece received her with: "What a blessed day this has been, Tía!"

"I have come to say goodbye, dear, for I must get back to the Academy."

"Before you leave, Tía, I want to tell you something. Do you know what has given me the greatest comfort in this hour of need? My devotion to Our Lady. My sins do not worry me at all. Tía, it is the love for the Blessed Virgin that you inspired in me as a Child of Mary that means everything to me now. . . . Tell the sodalists that one of them will have to come to take my place in the novitiate."

"I shall, Teresita. May Our Lady keep you! *Hasta la vista* and be brave, dear, . . ." Sister broke off; her unfinished words choked her.

"Don't be sad, Tía. I love suffering and I want more of it if God so desires. Perhaps by the time my last moment arrives I will have suffered enough to make my short life meritorious. I should like to die soon, Tía." Then, turning a frail face toward Our Lady's statue she ended, "But, dear Mother Mary, whatever you wish!"

It is easy to imagine the alarming impression that the final illness of their ideal produced on the Academy girls. Sister Teresa gave them a clear report and climaxed it with her niece's message to the sodalists. A few days later Teresita received the following letters from two of her former companions:

Dear Teresita: I am writing you this note because I want you to bring a message to Heaven for me. Please tell Our Blessed Lady to ask Our Lord to give me a vocation to the Carmelites of Charity. Please don't forget this. And also ask her to bless my family. Your former school chum, A. M.

The second letter ran:

Sister Teresa has told us about your illness and I am praying to Our Blessed Mother for you every day.

When you get to Heaven, ask Our Blessed Lady to help me be very good. The other day I was elected to the Sodality and with God's help I will be received in December.

Sister Teresa also told us you want one of us to take your place in the novitiate. I must tell you that I don't know what came over me the other day after receiving Holy Communion, but I promised to go to China as a missionary. I want to tell all those brothers and sisters of ours, who are living in the shadow of paganism, that there is a God in Heaven who watches over us. A God who came down to earth and loved us so much that He delivered Himself up to death in order to save us. I promise you, Teresita, to be faithful to God and to begin to do as much as I can to save souls. You from Heaven and I down here will work together for Christ, won't we? Now you know my secret; you are the first person I have told. Pray that I shall be able to go to China as soon as I graduate.

I know you will pray a great deal to Our Lady for me. Ask her to give me the strength to attain my ideal which, I think, is pleasing to her. Very affectionately, M.

After reading those letters Teresita looked up and saw her father standing in the doorway. "Oh, Papa, come in. How glad I am to see you! How is Mama?" she asked, as he embraced her.

"She is well and sends you much love. You must pray for your Mother, Teresita. She is suffering, in a way, more than you are."

"Mama will be all right. Her grief will last only until I reach Heaven. As soon as I meet God, I shall ask Him to send her complete resignation, Papa."

"Don't excite yourself, dear. Be tranquil. Perhaps I ought to. . . ."

"Papa," she interrupted, "if you were only half as tranquil as I am!"

How true! There were no signs of pain or of sickness, her father noticed. "You look well, today, Teresita."

"I am conquering, Papa. I am not going to die of this disease, thanks be to God! I am going to die of love, Papa."

As he smiled down upon her, Doctor Quevedo concluded that it was logical to believe that this child of God, so happy, so uncomplaining, so fearless, without preoccupations of any kind regarding her sickness, would die of love.

CHAPTER XVIII

A Spiritual Garden

Doctor and Mrs. Quevedo attended the Vocation Day Mass at Saint Francis Church on February 2, 1950. It was a happy coincidence that Father Lucas, S.J., had chosen "Novitiate" as the theme of his sermon rather than another of the many phases the word vocation suggests. Don Calixto was fascinated from the moment the Jesuit began.

There is no corner of the world where happiness is greater than in the novitiate of a religious community. In it the most pure and beautiful qualities of human life are harmonized: youth, chastity, love, sacrifice, obedience, joy and holy anticipation. No material worries invade its atmosphere of peace. There is no money, no family, no social life to disturb its serenity. In a way, there is no past; there is no future; it is like the eternal present. . . .

The young men and ladies who enter a monastery or a convent form a select society—a society picked by the hand of God. It is a society to whom He gives the same ideal, the same love, the same hope. These young people become the chosen family of God their Father and of Mary their Mother....

There is what we Jesuits call the time of the pin-prick—that epoch during which the novices' talents are exploited without indulgence of personal vanity. When their defects are made public without expression of discouragement or shame. When little needs suggest poverty. When the absence of a devoted family leads to a more intimate union with Christ....

The novitiate is a kingdom of silence and joy, of activity and calm, of the most complete subjection and of the most perfect liberty. No one does what he wants. But everyone does what he does because he wills it. A novice is incredibly poor but he lives in abundance....

After Mass Don Calixto and Doña María del Carmen went into the sacristy to commend Father Lucas, an old family friend, on his sermon.

"How good to see you again!" Father greeted them. "Thank you very much; I'm glad you found it an inspiring talk. If I had known you were in the congregation, I might have put in a word for the Carmelite Sisters of Charity," he said laughing. "How is Teresita, María del Carmen?"

"Would you like to see for yourself, Padre?" Don Calixto cut in. "Get your hat and we'll beg breakfast at Carabanchel. Carmen won't dare refuse you a few minutes with Teresita after we tell her of the boost you gave the novitiates this morning."

They drove off to Our Lady of Mount Carmel Novitiate. After the customary breakfast of coffee and fruit, Doctor Quevedo told Mother Carmen that he had really brought Father Lucas to visit Teresita.

"Of course, Calixto. Father's visit will be a spiritual treat for Teresita. Come with me, Father," Mother Carmen said, as she led him to the infirmary. The Quevedos remained in the guest dining room.

When his visit with Teresita ended, Father Lucas returned to the dining room, where the Quevedos were chatting with Mother Carmen. He wore a smile, and there was a pensive look in his eyes. Mother then sent Doctor and Mrs. Quevedo to the infirmary to greet their ailing daughter.

"Oh, Mama and Papa!" Teresita hugged each of them dearly. "This is the feast of Our Lady's Purification and she has sent me this unexpected joy! My happiness today will be complete, having seen you . . . and Father Lucas," she added as she saw him re-enter the infirmary. Mother Carmen was with him.

A brief exchange of words, Father Lucas' blessing, and the visitors were off.

As they drove back toward the center of Madrid, Father told Doctor and Mrs. Quevedo that he deeply appreciated the hour he had spent with Teresita. "There is just one little regret," he said. "I wish I had talked with her before I gave that sermon this morning. I would have done a better job by citing a few examples from her experiences. She is the most genuine novice I have ever known."

"Can you tell us why you say that, Padre?" Don Calixto was always anxious to learn more of the secrets of his little princess' soul.

"I don't know why not, Calixto; you don't want a blow by blow account of our conversation." He paused for a few moments, then continued: "Among other things, we discussed the Vows. I asked her a question on Chastity which she answered brilliantly. As an aftermath she added: 'That is the lily in my garden.' Your garden? I asked. 'Yes, Padre,' she answered. 'You see, I can best keep tabs on my spiritual progress by calling each virtue a flower, by planting it in my spiritual garden, watering it with prayer and penance, and watching its growth. I believe I took the idea from a passage in the *Life* of Saint Teresa of Avila that a holy Franciscan priest used as a conference theme when I was a senior at the Academy.'

" 'You were saying, Teresita, that the lily in your garden symbolizes chastity. What else grows in your spiritual garden?' I asked her. She was a little hesitant but continued: 'There are several, Padre. The white rose is charity; the red rose, mortification; the carnation represents poverty, and the forget-me-not, obedience. My precious violet signifies humility.'

"To probe a little further, I asked her why she called the violet precious. I noticed she hadn't any of the others. She answered directly: 'Because, Padre, the violet is the symbol of humility and since sanctity is impossible without it, the latter is precious indeed. Padre, I came here to become a saint. . . .' That is as far as she went, for she broke off when she heard your footsteps approaching the infirmary."

Doctor Quevedo pulled up at the door of the Jesuit college. He didn't turn off the engine. As Father Lucas hopped out of the car, the doctor said to him, "Teresita isn't the only one Our Lady has indulged on the feast of her purification. God bless you for sharing your visit with María del Carmen and me. Adiós, Padre."

Sister Jacinta tells us that in Teresita's final illness she was scrupulously careful not to waste anything, especially water.

Her concern for water, of course, could have been as much a natural as an acquired virtue. Castile is an arid land and water has always been a luxury there. So the natives of Madrid are schooled from childhood to use it sparsely.

"Teresita used to check me for wasting water on her ablutions, and so on," says Sister Jacinta. "Over and over again she said to me: 'You can say what you want about medical hygiene, Hermana, but that doesn't give you license to use two gallons of water where one will do the job.' She was sincere and, of course, correct."

When Teresita's appetite failed, Mother Carmen asked the dietician to prepare savory and dainty dishes, hoping to awaken in her a taste for nourishment. Sometimes she would nibble. Other times she left her tray untouched.

"It worried Teresita when she had to send the food back to the pantry for disposal," the nurse says. "She often commented on the waste and always lamented her inability to make public reparation in the refectory—(a penitential prayer said on one's knees during meals). 'If only I could share it with some hungry child!' she would say."

"My Beloved makes me feel the sting of poverty in very small ways, Madre," Teresita told Mother Carmen. "Nevertheless they are occasions to offer Him the perfume of my carnation."

Sister María Teresa loved her vow of chastity in a special way; thus she gave her lily particular care.

"I can still see Teresita," Sister Jacinta writes, "when I used to walk toward her bed to give her a bath. She never commented, but it cost her enormously to have me bathe her body when she was too weak to do it. I am sure she prayed as I bathed her, for her silence was indicative of something deeper than a natural modesty."

The third vow gave Sister María Teresa less concern. Perhaps her constant awareness of obedience suggested the name "forget-me-not." Obviously she never forgot it. She prayed to Our Lady "many times a day for the gift of 'blind obedience,' " she has told us.

Occasionally Teresita wondered how closely she would follow the letter of the law. For instance, when Reverend Mother General was making her visitation to the convents in Madrid in 1949, she visited Teresita in the infirmary. In the course of conversation Mother said: "Now let us see if you can glorify Our Blessed Mother with the miracle of a cure, Sister. I want you to be cured and I have ordered the Sisters to pray for it."

It was a dark moment for Teresita! Mother General "wanted a cure." Knowing this, how could she wish for Heaven? Obedience obliged her to submit to the will of her superiors.

Teresita's flexibility in the matter surprised everyone—even Sister Jacinta! She has related that after Mother left the infirmary, Teresita looked up at a picture of Our Lady that hung close to her bed and said: "If I should die now, having so recently made my vows, I would go directly to the arms of my Father in Heaven. But I will not ask that, dear Mother Mary; I ask only to please Jesus through you. How can I ask anything but the will of my superior, which is the will of God!"

Nevertheless, the desire for Heaven remained very much alive in Sister María Teresa of Jesus. There were moments when this knowledge distressed her, for she realized how determined Mother General was when she stated her desire for a miraculous cure. She did what any holy soul would—she followed the path obedience demanded. Teresita completely refrained from a further mention of death, and actually prayed for a cure.

Her humble submission could not go unrewarded. A visit from the Mother Provincial, whom Teresita loved, brought recompense to the little Sister. When they were alone in the infirmary, she confided to Mother the fears and desires of her heart, explaining in detail what the Mother General had said to her.

"I have prayed for the cure Mother General wants," Teresita stressed, "but Our Lady makes me feel that it was not meant to be a command."

"Of course not, Sister, and Mother General would not want you to interpret it that way," the kind Provincial comforted her. "Forget about that now, and tell me why you are so anxious to go to Heaven, Teresita."

"Because in Heaven I will adore God with Our Lady. Every moment will be one of rejoicing, of love, of praise, and of glory. In Heaven nothing will separate me from Jesus and Mary, Madre! Besides, I am of very little use here, but from Heaven you will see how busy I shall be."

CHAPTER XIX

New Sacrifice

NO ONE would have suspected that Teresita's headaches had become insufferable. She never complained. However, early in February, common sense told her to admit to her father: "Papa, if I don't get some relief, I am afraid these headaches will drive me out of my mind."

Looking into her feverish eyes, Don Calixto saw mirrored extreme agony—an agony that pierced his heart. "My child, a lumbar puncture is the only way to bring you relief. I will not do it, Teresita, but I shall call Doctor Lozano and ask him to come over immediately. It will be uncomfortable, but when the fluid which is causing the pain has been drawn off, you will feel a delightful relief. Your headache will be eased, if not cured. *Adiós,* my child!" He gently kissed her and hurried away to contact his colleague.

Today Teresita would have a new sacrifice to offer Our Lady. Alone for fifteen minutes, she prayed. Her colloquy was broken by the quick steps of Sister Jacinta, who entered the infirmary carrying a tray of sterile needles, syringes and test tubes. She placed them on a table near the bed.

"Doctor Lozano will be here shortly, Sister," the nurse announced. "I believe your father has told you that these lumbar punctures are not pleasant. Why don't you ask for an injection of novocain to deaden the pain? That is what your father gave you the day he took the specimen for the Laboratory. That was not an unpleasant experience. But if you don't have novocain for this lumbar puncture you will have dreadful pain."

Teresita did not answer Sister Jacinta. Her decision had been made a few minutes before. She would not submit to the soothing effect of a hypodermic because it would deny her the privilege of imitating her Crucified Savior!

"Good morning, Sister Jacinta. I know I am a little late, but a traffic jam on the Gran Via delayed me ten minutes. I asked Our Blessed Lady, finally, to clear the way and, don't you know, she did!" Turning to Teresita the doctor said: "Not feeling well today, Teresita, eh? We shall take care of that right now." Doctor Lozano washed his hands and put on a clinical coat. Then he bent his patient's fragile body into the posture necessary to administer the treatment.

"Gloves, Sister Jacinta, please?"

Sister flipped back the sterile cover of the tray.

Gloves adjusted, he picked up a four-inch needle and went to work.

When the ordeal was over, the nurse asked Teresita how she endured the pain. She answered: "*Hermanita,* I fixed my spiritual gaze on Calvary, contemplating the moment of Our Lord's passion when the spear pierced His sacred side. I knew, of course, that the spinal tap was but a pin-prick in comparison, but it was my 'widow's mite.' I offered it in reparation to God for the sins that are being committed against Divine Justice today."

Doctor Lozano was to puncture her spine sixty-four times.

The following day Dr. Quevedo and Dr. Lozano drove together to the novitiate at Carabanchel. On the way, they discussed the effects that the new antibiotics, which they were bringing to Teresita, might have upon the tuberculous meningitis. Each felt, although he did not express it, that if this medicine should arrest the progress of the disease, that was all it could do.

Mother Carmen received her brother and Doctor Lozano and took them directly to the Infirmary.

"Good morning, Princess. How do you feel today? Ready for a new antibiotic?" Doctor Quevedo greeted Teresita. He spoke with unaccustomed quickness, for he was trying to cover his emotions.

She smiled a greeting to Doctor Lozano, then turned to her father and said: "Papa, give me only enough medication to fulfill your obligation as a doctor. These antibiotics are going to delay my trip to Heaven, you know."

Teresita had been on the antibiotics for three days. Everyone had high hopes of a recovery, for her body seemed to be responding splendidly. In mid-February Mother Carmen was confident of a cure—so confident that she wrote the following letter to her sisters in Puerto Rico:

It looks as if God is going to leave our little angel with us. She is responding beautifully to the new medicine. It may not please Teresita to recover, but it will certainly be a joy to the Community and to her good parents. Of late she has had restful nights. She sleeps from ten until after one o'clock. Then the nurse gives her a sedative which puts her to sleep until about six-thirty. For the past week she has not suffered severely because the new medicine has finally brought great relief, thank God.

You will remember I wrote you that it had absolutely no effect in the beginning. Continue to pray that God's holy will may be fulfilled in her.

Teresita, however, did not abandon her fervent desire to meet Our Lady in Heaven. She could not be convinced that she was improving physically. "I don't know how they can say that I am getting better, because my body tells me the contrary," she told her nurse.

In spite of herself, the doctors managed to convince Teresita that she was improving. The nuns helped by assuring her that their campaign of prayer was obtaining a miraculous cure. She didn't like to admit it, but she knew she was no worse.

"You are all trying to change the plan of God," she said jocosely to her father. "If He should cure me, Papa, then I will consider this a forewarning that I shall become a saint at some later day. For when we reach Heaven, we shall be sanctified. But I am afraid that you are going to leave me without a miracle and without Heaven too." Her good humor was a tonic to her father.

"Now tell me, Teresita, why are you in such a hurry to get to Heaven? For your mother's sake alone, you should not desire to leave us as you do."

"Oh, Papa, do not worry about Mama. I have told you many times that, as I enter Heaven, Our Lady will shower her own comfort on Mama. You will see, Papa!"

"All right, Princess, we shall see! Did I tell you that I was speaking with Father Valentin Sanchez? He is delighted about your progress. He said that when you are cured, you can do a great deal of good because of the deep love—the vocation—you have for the missions."

"That makes me happy, Papa. But if, as you think, I have

the capacity to do so much good on earth, imagine what I should be able to do from Heaven!"

Was there anything that could awaken in Teresita a desire to live? he wondered. He recalled a recent conversation he had had with Sister Teresa, the Sodality Prefect at the Academy. This may do it, he thought. "It is difficult to understand your longing to go to Heaven, Teresita, since by living longer, you could teach many souls to love Our Blessed Lady."

Teresita did not respond with her accustomed rapidity. She looked seriously into her father's eyes for a few moments. Finally she answered, "Papa, I should like very much to teach many souls on earth to love Our Lady; but I can only repeat that I do not believe it is God's will for me to teach them here to love His Mother. From her side in Heaven, Papa, I will teach many to love Our Lady with abandon, and to go to Our Lord through her."

The wise minds of the Church teach us that sickness does not alter man but rather shows him what he is. It may bring to light unknown virtue, or it may unveil defects which in his ordinary life are not always manifest. The period of illness can also be a time of spiritual harvest, as it was with Teresita Quevedo. During her brief years of health, she had constantly sown seeds of amiability. They were bound to produce a rich crop of charity when her hour of need was at hand.

"During her last illness," remarked Sister Rosario Prieto, "no matter how ill Teresita felt, she was always solicitous about the affairs of those who visited her. She used to invite visitors to sit and chat. If her suffering mounted, she would force herself to smile and to carry on a jovial conversation. One would think she felt wonderfully well. If at times someone would suggest that she rest while they sat with her, she would reply: 'It is impossible, *Hermanita;* I am not tired.' Sister María Teresa never let pass an occasion to sanctify herself."

The novices studied Teresita's virtue as faithfully as they read their Holy Rule. Not a day passed without a visit to the infirmary. "We could not resist, in spite of our determination not to disturb her," said one of her sister novices. "Her smile alone left us with a spiritual satisfaction that we could not otherwise have known. Teresita taught us lesssons of solid virtue from her sick bed."

A young professed Sister, crippled and quite incapacitated, frequently stopped at the infirmary to unburden her soul to Teresita. She was not resigned to her cross, for she found her uselessness beyond her natural capacity to bear. Sister María Teresa's heart had always ached for this nun, for she understood her trials. A day arrived, however, when Sister María Teresa realized that it would be a charity to tell Sister what God really expected of her. Teresita asked Mother Carmen to send that Sister to the infirmary. After a prudent approach to the subject, Teresita said with an affectionate but firm tone, *"Hermanita,* you will have to try to sanctify your life by being patient with the cross God has asked you to carry. Don't you realize that you can save many souls through patience?" As if to relieve any offense she may have incurred, she added, "I believe I am going to Heaven soon. From there I hope to do a great deal of good for the Institute, for the world and for you, too, *Hermana."*

The crippled nun told her confessor about Teresita's kind words. She concluded with: "I had always admired her virtue, Padre, for it edified me. But as I sat at her bedside, listening to her counsel and her promise, I felt as if Our Lady were directing the words to me. I went to chapel when I left Sister

María Teresa and promised God never to complain again of my uselessness."

"What is the matter, Sister?" the anguish in Sister Jacinta's voice rang through the infirmary. Teresita, pale as death, was kneeling upright in bed, her arms stretched out toward the crucifix that hung on the wall over the bedstead.

"Nothing, *Hermanita,*" she answered, slowly dropping her arms. "Mother told me this morning how seriously ill the new postulant is, so I have just asked a favor of our Crucified Lord. Since I am already gravely ill and have made my vows, I have asked Christ to relieve the postulant by adding her illness to mine. If He hears me, she will be well soon, and I will suffer more for my Beloved."

God accepted Teresita's generosity. Two days later, the postulant was pronounced well by the doctor. Mother Carmen, knowing of her niece's generous sacrifice, brought the recovered postulant to the infirmary. Teresita was suffering agonies of pain that day—she was scarcely able to move. However, she managed a smile and whispered: "Now you can work for Christ, *Hermanita.* God reward you for this visit!"

Later the same day, two Sisters from the Academy called to see Teresita, shortly after she had passed a terrible siege of pain. She extended her hand and greeted them as if nothing serious had happened prior to their visit. Mother Carmen, observing her niece, said, "Don't converse at length, Sisters; Teresita has just suffered quite an ordeal. We must not cause an upset stomach or a rise in temperature by exerting her."

Sister María Teresa tried to take the importance out of Mother's words by answering, "Mother, it is not as extreme as that. The Sisters will think I am a martyr." During that visit she not only smiled as if it were "not as extreme as that," but she conversed with a fluency that caused Mother Carmen to shake her head in wonder.

Sister Jacinta's devotion to Teresita was remarked by everyone at Carabanchel. Although she enjoyed the reputation of being an excellent and very kind nurse, they had never before seen her so attentive to a patient. "I wonder why Sister Jacinta never gives anyone else a chance to spend the evening recreation period with Teresita? She always recreates with her," a novice commented one evening in the novitiate.

"Undoubtedly Sister María Teresa prefers that Sister Jacinta sit with her," said a brand new postulant who thought she had the answers to all questions.

The novices' reaction was like a clap of rolling thunder. The shocked postulants looked from one to another. What had she said? It was not until Sister María Zaboleta, who presided at that recreation, had quieted them down that the postulant realized her imprudence.

"When you have lived with us longer, my dear little Sister, you will learn something of the virtue of Sister María Teresa." Sister María Zaboleta directed that remark to the postulant. Then to everyone present she said: "When Sister María Teresa was first taken ill, I used to wonder why she did not ask more frequently for visits from Mother Carmen, or Sister Teresa, on her novice-companions. One day I questioned her about it. She admitted that her affection for her aunts was great. She admitted, too, that she loved some of the novices more than others. 'But,' she concluded, 'I could not displease Our Lord by requesting particular visitors; I prefer to entertain those He sends me.' "

CHAPTER XX

Saturday of Glory

ON MONDAY, Mother Carmen instructed the novices on the ceremonies for the last four days of Holy Week. Afterwards, she read the list of convent duties for the general Easter housecleaning that would begin immediately. As she was about to dismiss them, the Mistress of Postulants whispered to her that Sister Ana María had not been given a charge. She was an ailing, sensitive soul and to forget her was the last thing Mother wanted to do.

"Sister Ana María," Mother said, referring to her paper as if the charge were written there, "you will relieve Sister Jacinta in the infirmary this week whenever she is needed elsewhere. Come with me now and I'll give you an embroidery piece to work on while you sit with the sick. If you finish it by Holy Saturday, we shall give it to Doctor Lozano as a gift from the novices. Now, see what I have done! Sister Ana María has two charges rather than the usual one."

"Thank you, Mother," Sister replied. She tried to replace with a smile the frown that marked her embarrassment, but she was unsuccessful.

An hour later Sister Jacinta's services were needed in the cell of an aging sister. Sister Ana María, embroidery in hand, seated herself in Teresita's room.

Teresita knew nothing of the charge imposed upon Sister Ana María when she asked, "*Hermanita,* are you going to remain for a visit with me?"

Still nursing her humiliation, the young nun answered tersely, "I have to, at the request of Mother Mistress. Like you, I am forced to shun the preparations for Easter."

Such a reply was wholly unexpected and it hurt Teresita. "Shun the preparations," she thought, "so that is the wound!" Looking Sister directly in the eye she asked, "Well, why did you come to the novitiate, *Hermana,* to busy yourself with 'preparations' or to sanctify yourself?"

Sister Ana María's failure to respond drew a softened but strong explanation from Teresita.

"God asks each one of us to sanctify herself in a different way, *Hermana.* At the moment He wants that of you, and this illness of me. Do you think it will please Him if we sulk about it? God only asks us to supply what we lack in body with a generous and loving spirit. Then when the day of your Profession arrives, if someone should say: 'She seems too sickly to be professed,' many others will be able to defend your cause by saying: 'She is gracious, generous, and observant of the Holy Rule. She has the spirit of her state and should be professed.' To obtain such virtue you must place your confidence in the Blessed Virgin Mary. Didn't you enter during her month? And wasn't it only after surmounting untold obstacles that they admitted you to her Institute, *Hermanita?*"

It seemed like an hour to Teresita, but it was really only five minutes—five minutes of deep thinking on Sister Ana's part—before a humbled and grateful voice replied, "How could I have been so blind? God reward you, Sister María Teresa! I resented this charge when Mother assigned it, but now I see it as a special Easter gift from Our Lord . . . the most perfect He could have given me! O Teresita, I am so ashamed of my selfishness! Please beg Our Crucified Savior to forgive me and to teach me His humility. I shall always be grateful to you for helping me find myself."

It was a wonderful initiation into one of the most solemn moments of the ecclesiastical year for Sister Ana María and Teresita. Both rejoiced in different ways! Sister Ana was grateful to Teresita. Teresita spoke her gratitude to Our Lady. And as Monday lengthened into Tuesday each knew that *it* was only the beginning of a steady flow of grace that would penetrate her soul on that glorious Easter of Holy Year.

Teresita grew gravely ill the following day. Every bone in her body ached, the pain in her head increased; nausea was frequent and violent; her temperature rose alarmingly. The doctors noticed a tremendous change for the worse and ordered Sister Jacinta to keep visitors from the room.

Teresita's sufferings were assuaged by the comfort that came from her love for Our Lady. Alone most of the time, she conversed with her. *"How deeply I suffer,"* she would tell her. *"All for you, sweet Lady. All for Jesus through my Mother Mary. . . . Sweet Lady, I am very sick. I offer you this illness. . . . I trust in you, Mary, my Mother. . . . Mary, my Mistress, I obey you. . . . I love you, Queen of my heart!"*

She was clear in her prayer, but her conversation with Sister Jacinta betrayed a confused mind. "She could not understand," said Sister, "why my head did not ache. Repeatedly she asked me if I felt any relief. I suppose her intense agony produced a delirium in which she thought I was the patient."

Shortly before night prayers that evening, her father and Doctor Lozano called at the infirmary. Teresita greeted them with a smile and looked long and inquiringly at her father.

"We have come to give you a nightcap, Teresita," said Dr. Lozano, laughing and producing a hypodermic. "You must have a good night. Reverend Mother orders it!"

Obedience! Submission! *"Bueno,* Doctor, thank you." Then she turned her sweet glance toward her father and said: "Good-night, Papa. Give me your blessing."

On Wednesday morning Teresita was extremely lethargic and unresponsive—apparently in a coma. Reverend Mother thought it wise, therefore, to have the professed Sisters, two every hour, keep vigil at her bedside.

The nuns on watch late in the afternoon were certain that Teresita's closed eyes and motionless figure indicated either coma or profound slumber. Softly Sister Monica commented: "Isn't it a pity that Mother Carmen has to give poor little Sister María Bañegas such sad news at a time when all hearts are preparing to celebrate Easter."

"It is indeed," was the reply. "It would not be such a blow if she had been expecting her mother's death. . . ."

"What happened, *Hermanas?*" the thin voice of Teresita broke in and her eyes, resembling two tiny balls of fire, were fastened on the nuns.

The Sisters looked at each other utterly surprised. What would Mother Carmen think of them? It was too late now, for there was no alternative; they would have to tell her.

"We thought you were asleep, dear," said the senior of the two nuns, "or we shouldn't have mentioned the sudden death of Sister Bañegas' mother. However, since you are so close to

God perhaps Mother Carmen won't mind our telling you. She died suddenly, early this morning. Recommend her soul to God, Sister, for He will listen to whatever petitions you make Him."

Teresita closed her eyes. For a long time the Sister watched her lips moving in prayer. Finally she fell into a sleep of exhaustion.

Twilight in pink-purple streams was flooding the infirmary when Teresita awoke to find the nun keeping vigil at her bedside none other than Mother Carmen. Forgetting her sufferings she smiled up at Mother and asked with sincere interest, "Madre, how is poor Sister Bañegas? Please tell her that I am praying and offering my pain for her Mother's eternal repose. And tell her, too, that I am begging Our Blessed Lady to be her Mother doubly . . . doubly now!" That was as much as she could say; weakness overpowered her and she again went into a coma.

Holy Thursday was a day of extreme rejoicing at Carabanchel. Aside from the beautiful spiritual significance it holds for the Catholic world, especially for those consecrated to God, it brought a new joy, a new hope. Sister María Teresa showed remarkable improvement. It was almost unbelievable. The gravely ill patient of yesterday sat up in bed and ate a normal meal. She chatted lightly, laughed gaily, and prayed profoundly.

At six o'clock, after a long nap, Teresita asked Sister Jacinta to bring her a snack. The nurse hesitated for a moment, then recalling that Doctor Lozano said she was to have anything she wished, she brought her steaming chocolate and assorted cookies.

Sitting high in her bed, supported by a bower of pillows, Teresita began to sip the chocolate. Sister Jacinta sat beside her. She had just made a mental note of her patient's flushed face when a sudden, sharp cry brought her to her feet. It was Teresita. Trembling like a leaf, she tried to speak but could not. In a split second she fell, pale as death, into unconsciousness.

It was only a matter of minutes until Teresita's father and Doctor Lozano were at her bedside. Their expression told the nurse that the fulfillment of their fears was at hand. Reality had utterly crushed hope.

"Let us give her what relief we can, Lozano," her father said.

Silently, valiantly, Dr. Lozano prepared to give her a spinal tap. But even with reason inert, Teresita defended herself against the needle with the strength that frequently empowers a worn body before death. She protested utterly. There was nothing left for Dr. Lozano to do but to apply the less potent remedies that science suggests for the dulling of pain that cannot be permanently relieved . . . for the retarding of a death that cannot be avoided.

Teresita rallied and regained consciousness but she was not the same: her eyes were less bright; her words, less spontaneous; her mind, less clear. She was not the same physically, yet she was never more herself in that which constituted the essence of her life. Her love for Our Lady was strong, tender, complete.

"The words she spoke to Our Lady as I sat with her," wrote Sister María Segura, "are words I shall never forget: *'My dear Mother Mary, I have tried to be perfect for your sake. . . . Now you will take me with you to Heaven. . . . My Jesus, I love You for those who do not love You. . . . My Mother, I would rather die a thousand times than offend you once. . . . Jesus, I have loved only You and my dear Mother Mary.'* That last visit with Teresita made me think deeply. There she lay on the eve of death, crucial pain overpowering her already broken and frail body, yet she did not complain. She forgot herself completely and sought only to please Our Lady and to give glory to God. To me it was a proof of what we have been taught since our earliest days in religion: as you live, so shall you die."

The night was a long, hallowed one for those who prayed for and watched the agonies of Teresita. After that six o'clock attack her neck remained rigid and she was not able to turn her head without suffering pain. Incoherent words formed an Act of Spiritual Communion which she repeated many times throughout the night: *"My Lord, . . . here is one . . . who loves You . . . and desires . . . ardently . . . to receive You."* Broken words bespoke a complete holocaust to our Lady: *"I am all yours. . . . O my Mother, . . . for you I was born . . . for you I die. . . . What do you wish . . . my Mother . . . of me? I am all yours . . . all yours . . . all yours. . . . O Mother of love, . . . cover me . . . with your . . . mantle of blue. . . ."*

At intervals, alternate thoughts of her goal in the active religious life and of her affection for her beloved sister Carmen would crowd her turbulent brain and she would beg, *"O my God . . . send workers . . . to the missions . . . more workers. . . ."* Then: *"Carmencita . . . how beautiful . . . she is. How good . . . she is. . . ."*

It must have been a beautifully pleasing sight to Almighty God that Holy Thursday night as He looked down upon the novitiate of the Carmelite Sisters of Charity in Madrid, where He beheld His little victim soul and her novice companions. Teresita did not sleep. From her cloistered bed she adored Christ throughout the night in disconnected expressions of love that yielded her soul unreservedly to Him. The novices spoke their love in adoration of the Most Blessed Sacrament in the chapel Repository below. How sincerely they begged the Eucharistic King to attain the fulfillment of the Heavenly Father's will in Teresita!

There was every indication that Christ intimately shared His Good Friday with Sister María Teresa. She suffered as never before! Divine Providence ordained that she remain fully conscious the entire day. Thus she entered more fully into the Passion of Our Lord. The morning passed calmly enough, but the agonies of the early afternoon caused Reverend Mother to believe that the end was near. A priest anointed the suffering nun. As frequently happens, Extreme Unction brought new strength to her body.

Her soul, too, became fortified for final struggles against the attacks of Satan. The latter's fury over the complete war her soul had constantly waged on him was made evident by the manner in which he marauded the infirmary. Sister Jacinta heard Teresita punctuate her pious aspirations many times with: *"Go away from me. . . . Begone Satan! . . . Go back to hell. . . ."* When his attacks were too violent, she would ask Sister to pray with her: *"Defend me, O Mary, defend me against the snares of the devil."*

Sister María Zaboleta relieved the nurse for collation in the evening. Teresita seemed to be excessively restless. Suddenly Sister María realized that Teresita was suffering a diabolical attack. It was the nun's first experience with a soul visibly tortured by Satan and she did not know what to do until reason dominated her emotions. Together they prayed aloud. When they invoked the name of Jesus, Sister María sprinkled holy water in the direction of Teresita's pointed finger and the devil fled from his little victim.

It took all the courage she had to appear unshaken, but Sister María felt it her duty to comment on those onslaughts. . . . "God permits such torments, Sister, only to provide you with greater opportunities to gain merit for Heaven. Do not be too upset about them. . . ."

"I am not at all annoyed about his attacks, Sister," the patient answered with deep humility and conviction. She seemed stronger as she continued: "I know he will not be able to disturb me with his diabolical talk when the hour of death arrives, because I shall be in Our Blessed Lady's arms." After a pause she concluded: "I have gathered great strength from the words of Saint Bonaventure: 'Those who constantly invoke the name of Mary need not fear the hour of death, because at the sound of her name the infernal spirits flee terrified.' "

A long silent period followed during which Sister María watched Teresita press her temples as if to force pain from her head; or she would stretch her arms back to grasp the iron bars of the bedstead and, pressing her elbows against her brow with all the strength she had, she would attempt to deaden the pain in her head. As the evening lengthened, her suffering became intensified. Her soul, however, continued to sing a canticle of love: *"My Lord . . . my God, . . . my All! . . . I love You. . . . All for Thee, . . . Sweet Jesus, . . . I am all Yours. . . . My beloved to me, and I to my Beloved. . . . Mary . . . Jesus . . . Love."*

Sister María had never felt so closely in touch with the Divine as she did that Good Friday night.

April eighth, Holy Saturday, dawned fresh and new with all the effulgence that Holy Mother Church places in her ceremonies. The Spaniards call it *Sabado de Gloria* and it was a Saturday of Glory indeed for Teresita . . . of Glory that would never end.

Doctor Quevedo attended six o'clock Mass at the Carthusian Monastery so as to be able to visit his princess early in the morning. When he reached Carabanchel the Community

Mass was about to begin and it was his happy privilege to keep vigil with his loving child while Sister Jacinta attended Mass. Teresita's eyes were closed and she made no sign of recognition as he tenderly kissed her forehead. There were a few incoherent words at intervals and then she opened her eyes and looked about searchingly. Her father's heart beat quickly. When recognition set in, she smiled at him and feebly extending her hand, she tried to squeeze his affectionately as she said, "Papa, I am very ill today." Then she closed her eyes again and seemed to sleep.

"She talked very little but smiled a great deal," said Doctor Quevedo. "Whenever she spoke, it was in praise of her Divine Creator. She appeared joyful and serene in spite of the disease that had almost completely consumed her body. The pain in her head was intolerable and it took all the courage I had to stand there and watch her suffer, but there was nothing further medicine could do. As the day wore on, her restlessness increased and the pain grew steadily worse. She could not help her cries of 'Oh, what agony!' but she managed to offer each attack to God by following it with: 'All for Thee . . . Sweet Jesus!' She was an inspiration to me and to all who saw her."

Toward evening Doctor Lozano told Reverend Mother María Gonzalez that it would be well to recite the prayers for the dying, according to custom. Mother summoned the Community and as they gathered in the infirmary they noticed that Teresita lay as if in a peaceful sleep. Reverend Mother intoned the Litany for a Happy Death and, while the nuns were answering "pray for her," they heard Teresita, with the most perfect serenity, saying "pray for me."

The prayers for the dying of the Institute are very long. Fearing they would exhaust Teresita if they should say them in their entirety, Reverend Mother paused after the act of immolation to Our Lady and whispered in her ear: "Sister Maria Teresa, I am afraid we are tiring you, so we are going to leave you now."

Without answering, Teresita reached out and tried feebly to open Mother's prayer book. Her nod, as she did so, told Mother to continue the prayers to the end.

They stopped again, after having completed the exact number of supplications. A novice entered the room and knelt to tell Mother Carmen that Teresita's aunt was calling Mother on the telephone. Teresita evidently overheard the novice's message, for as Mother whispered a reply, Teresita pleaded: "Do not leave me, Madrecita! Give me your blessing." She opened her arms as if to embrace her dear aunt.

The Community filed out. Mother Carmen, profoundly touched by her niece's final display of affection, begged the benediction of God to descend upon her. Then she leaned over Teresita and said in a soft tone: "You love Our Lord very much!"

"For Him alone have I lived," Teresita answered with the full fervor of her soul.

"My dear child, pray constantly for the Institute when you get to Heaven. Pray for all the Sisters so that we may never seriously fail in charity." Then Mother repeated over and over the ejaculations which she knew were dear to her niece's heart: "Sacred Heart of Jesus, I trust in You! Look compassionately upon me, dearest Mother, and do not leave me."

Teresita was sinking rapidly. At ten forty-five Holy Saturday night she uttered a painful cry. It caused the Mothers who sat praying beside her to fear that an attack similar to that of Holy Thursday was about to overtake her. "My Jesus, mercy!"... "Help me, dearest Mother Mary!" Mother Carmen alternately whispered in her ear. When the Sisters around her bed believed she was no longer conscious of her aunt's pleas to Heaven, Teresita opened her eyes wide and, with a voice that filled the room she said, *"My Mother, Mary, come for me. Bring me back to Heaven with you!"*

The Community was summoned. As they filed into the infirmary they knelt about her bed. Reverend Mother made one last plea for a miracle. Rubbing the relic of their Holy Foundress, Joaquina de Vedruna, on Teresita's brow, she said, "Sister María Teresa, ask Our Lady to restore you to perfect health."

With a clear voice, Teresita answered: *"My Mother . . . whatever you wish!"* She tightly clasped in her right hand the little reliquary that Mother had placed on her heart. Looking up with wide eyes, an angelic smile on her face, she said, *"How beautiful! O Mary, how beautiful you are!"*

Every nun kneeling about her bed had but one thought: Does Teresita see Our Lady?

Sister María Teresa's hands fell heavily from her chest upon the bed. Her lips still moved in silent prayer. Mother Carmen raised a crucifix to them and she kissed it several times with visible fervor. A few minutes later, Mother held Teresita's favorite picture of the Blessed Virgin before her. The response was a deep sigh after which her eyes remained fixed and expressionless.

How could Mother doubt it? If Sister María Teresa of Jesus had failed to kiss Our Lady's picture it was because her soul was no longer captive in her body. Teresita had begged: "My Mother, come for me," and the Queen and Love of her life, indulging her child to the end, responded to that call.

CHAPTER XXI

Easter Aura

REVEREND Mother asked Mother Carmen to break the news of Teresita's death to her family. Early Easter Sunday morning she called Calixto's number. She thought she detected an ominous note in the voice that said: "Doctor Quevedo's residence."

"This is Carmen, . . ." she began.

Teresita's mother interrupted, "Carmen, I know you are going to tell me that Our Lady has taken Teresita to Heaven."

"Yes, María del Carmen," she answered. Their conversation revealed Mrs. Quevedo's absolute resignation to God's holy will. She edified Mother Carmen. "Is Calixto there?" she asked.

"Hello, Carmen." Doctor Quevedo's voice was natural. "What time did our angel go to meet her Divine Lord?"

"At five minutes to eleven, Calixto."

"God's will is our will. Why didn't you call me last night, Carmen?"

"I wanted to, but Reverend Mother decided against it. You had a strenuous day, Calixto, and you needed a night of uninterrupted rest." Mother tried to cloak the emotion in her voice with naturalness as she added: "There will be a Solemn High Easter Mass at eight. Reverend Mother would like the four of you to attend. Please come, Calixto; I would like to see you and the family. There are some beautiful details regarding Teresita's last moments with us that will bring deep peace to your soul."

When Doctor Quevedo and his family entered the convent chapel, the novices' choir was singing "Rejoice, O Queen of Heaven, alleluia!, because your Son has risen from the dead, alleluia!" As they filed into the pew reserved for them, varied emotions filled the hearts of Teresita's family. Carmen and Luis wondered how those novices could sing so joyously if they had loved Sister María Teresa as it was said they did. More mature thoughts consoled the doctor and his wife. They knew, in a way only truly spiritual parents can know, that their child had reached the heights of happiness and love. They realized, too, that Teresita was only lent to them by God in order to accomplish the brief mission He had ordained for her on earth. Moreover, it was Holy Year and beyond the ever ancient, ever new glory of Christ's Resurrection, the Queen of Teresita's heart had brought another Holy Year joy to Heaven.

"Victoria, victoria! Surrexit nostra gloria! Alleluia, alleluia! . . ." The Mass was ended.

The Easter sun was high in the heavens when Teresita's body was presented for viewing in the long salon opposite the chapel in the novitiate building. She was dressed in the habit of a professed sister, crowned with roses, the symbolic lily mounted on her Rule in one hand, and the crucifix in the other. Teresita was beautiful in death. There is no adequate manner of describing what viewers saw in her corpse. Some observed a delicate face with the trace of a benign smile. Others saw majesty, or simplicity, or holy peace. A Jesuit friend of her Uncle Antonio said, as he looked at Teresita in the coffin: "Even in death, she teaches us a philosophy of life, perhaps more eloquent in its silence than the exhorting of a hundred preachers in as many years."

A steady stream of relatives, friends and classmates called to pay their last respects to a loved, admired and mourned Teresita. Few passed the coffin without touching a pair of rosary beads, a medal or a scapular to the body. Reverend Mother did not favor it, but there was little she could do about it, for the professed nuns had set the example.

The novices, who knew Teresita well, brought their copy of the Holy Rule to the viewing. In turn, each placed it near Sister María Teresa's heart and whispered a brief prayer in passing. Perhaps they asked: "Pray that we may keep the Rule as you have always kept it."

Had the interest in Teresita and the enthusiasm regarding her holiness died with the eulogies that were delivered and the letters that were written at her death, perhaps she would have remained hidden from the world. Time, however, did not eradicate her memory. As it passed, she became known not only on the Spanish Peninsula, but also in many parts of Europe and America. Her holiness was honored by outstanding personages of the Church. Cardinals, archbishops, bishops, monsignori, priests and religious sent messages of hope that she would soon be glorified with the honors of the Church.

The humble little Sister who had never seen her name in print would have blushed to read the words of Toledo's Archbishop, Dr. Pla y Daniel, Primate of Spain. He wrote an article, published in the Catholic periodical "Reason and

Faith," which reads in part: "May God grant that Teresita Quevedo serve as an example to the youth of our day.... May her life be an inspiration and a source of encouragement to all those who follow a vocation to fulfill God's will perfectly in their life.... Like a meteor of holiness, this humble girl has pierced the heavens because of her strong devotion to Our Blessed Lady.... She has become a new flower of the Church.... She was a valuable gift from God to our beloved Country.... Let us petition God fervently for the glorification of this chaste soul who, from her Mother's side in Heaven, will steal many souls for the Church...."

There are dozens and dozens of commentaries on the Marian devotion of Sister María Teresa of Jesus which, if they were not repetitious, would make a sizable volume of interesting reading.

Radio Nacional, National Broadcasting Company of Spain, broadcast a program on twentieth century holiness to all of Western Europe a few years ago. Teresita Quevedo's life was summarized on the program, whose aim it was to prove that "holiness is not a stumbling block in the normal life of a modern girl." The remarkable words that concluded the broadcast were: "We are better in heart and in soul for having known Teresita Quevedo. We feel a little closer to God, perhaps, because of the urge she has given us to imitate her strong qualities of moral balance and her love for the Mother of God. Teresita's way of life is in no way contrary to the ordinary Christian's pattern of life, for all of us are called to sanctity. *"Be ye perfect,"* Christ tells us, *"as your Heavenly Father is perfect."*

CHAPTER XXII

Fulfillment

THE steadfast devotion to Our Blessed Lady which made Sister María Teresa of Jesus' life one swift ascent to Jesus through Mary has reaped the desired rewards for those she held most dear during her life on earth.

In the Spring of 1959, Doctor Quevedo was rushed to the hospital in Madrid gravely ill and suffering violent pain. The diagnosis? A ruptured ulcer. Immediate surgery followed—and a prognosis that was not hopeful. The day after the operation, in answer to Don Calixto's inquiry concerning the truth of his condition, the surgeon told him that he was on the critical list. Only God could bring him recovery. Doctor Quevedo made no response. Perhaps because at that moment he recalled something Teresita had said to him many times, when he had chided her about her desire for an early death. Later in the day, he said to his grieved wife: "Don't be alarmed, María del Carmen. My princess in heaven will come to our rescue." And she did! Teresita had meant it when she said: "Papa, you must not jest about my wish to die. Some day you will know how much I shall be able to do from my heavenly home."

Doña María del Carmen certainly won the "comforting touch of Our Lady" to which Teresita so frequently referred. It was prevalent in her complete and holy resignation to God's will on that Easter Sunday morning in 1950 when she heard of her daughter's death. Again, after her husband's recent recovery, we note the consolation that Teresita has brought to her mother's soul. On June 10, 1959, Doña María del Carmen wrote the following in a letter to a friend in America: "The clouds on life's horizon are so quickly dispersed when I recall the love my angelic Teresita had for Our Blessed Mother. It has taught me to accept the ups and downs of everyday life—as well as a cross as heavy to bear as Calixto's recent illness—with love and courage. . . ."

We recall Teresita's deep desires for Luis' success at engineering school. How happy and proud she would have been could she have seen his name when it appeared on a current roster of Madrid's outstanding engineers!

Her dear Carmen is blissfully married to Javier. They live in Madrid, the parents of a delightful family.

In 1951, a Spanish biography of Sister María Teresa of Jesus was published in Madrid under the title of *Teresita.* It embodies a preface, written by the Bishop of Ciudad Rodrigo, which merits a place in this, the first English biography of Teresita Quevedo. The Bishop wrote:

> The book which you have in your hands is not one to leaf through and set aside for someone else to read. That God has placed it in your hands should be sufficient to assure you that there is something in it written just for you.
>
> If you are a man, prepare yourself to enter into a beautiful and chaste feminine world.

If you are a father, the intimacy of the authentic Christian family sketched on these pages will delight you.

If you are a woman . . . there are a million things in this book for you.

If you are a young girl, walking the same path as that of Teresita, it will fascinate you.

If you are a young Religious, you could be the protagonist.

Whoever you are, read to the end and you will learn how a holy and happy young girl finds God.

Jesus, Bishop of Ciudad Rodrigo.

Three years after the publication of that book—during the 1954 Marian Year—an investigation into the virtue and the holy life of Sister María Teresa of Jesus was organized and directed by the Primate of Spain, Cardinal Pla y Daniel. Four years of intensive study brought the investigation to a close on December 27, 1958. One month later, on January 29, 1959, two Carmelite Sisters of Charity left Madrid bound for Rome. They went at the instruction of His Eminence the Cardinal Primate of Spain to present Sister María Teresa's Cause for beatification to the Sacred Congregation of Rites, where it is now under examination.